‘This is one of the most profound and transformative creative projects I’ve ever encountered: I felt both completely devastated and completely renewed by it. Birthed from and through a genocide, *The Nightmare Sequence* is an astonishingly original collaboration by two artists who are committed to the intimacies of humanity, the details of injustice, and uncompromising truth-telling. In a world that has rejected the Arab as being worthy of life and dignity, read this book to be reminded of the generosity and love of artists who insist on bearing witness to the trauma and humanity of Palestinians.’ **Randa Abdel-Fattah**

Omar Sakr is a poet and writer born in Western Sydney to Lebanese and Turkish Muslim migrants. He is the acclaimed author of the novel *Son of Sin* and three poetry collections, including *The Lost Arabs*, which won the 2020 Prime Minister's Literary Award for Poetry. His most recent collection, *Non-Essential Work*, was shortlisted for the Kenneth Slessor Prize and the ALS Gold Medal. His non-fiction work has been published widely, including in *The Guardian*, *The Sydney Morning Herald* and *SBS Life*.

Safdar Ahmed is an award-winning artist, writer, musician and cultural worker. His graphic novel *Still Alive* won the Multicultural NSW Award and was named Book of the Year in the 2022 NSW Premier's Literary Awards. *Still Alive* also won the 2022 Eve Pownall Award and a Gold Ledger in the 2022 Comic Arts Awards of Australia. Safdar is a founding member of the Refugee Art Project and a member of *eleven*, a collective of contemporary Muslim Australian artists, curators and writers.

THE NIGHTMARE SEQUENCE

Omar Sakr &
Safdar Ahmed

UQP

First published 2025 by University of Queensland Press
PO Box 6042, St Lucia, Queensland 4067 Australia

The University of Queensland Press (UQP) acknowledges the Traditional Owners and their custodianship of the lands on which UQP operates. We pay our respects to their Ancestors and their descendants, who continue cultural and spiritual connections to Country. We recognise their valuable contributions to Australian and global society.

uqp.com.au
reception@uqp.com.au

Cover design by Josh Durham, Design by Committee
Cover images: 'Despair' (front) and 'Rescuers' (back and spine) by Safdar Ahmed
Typeset in 12.5/16.5 pt Adobe Garamond Pro by Post Pre-press Group, Brisbane

Printed in Australia by McPherson's Printing Group

University of Queensland Press is assisted by the Australian Government through Creative Australia, its principal arts investment and advisory body.

University of Queensland Press is assisted by the Queensland Government through Arts Queensland.

This project is supported by the NSW Government through Create NSW.

A catalogue record for this book is available from the National Library of Australia.

ISBN 978 0 7022 6890 8 (pbk)
ISBN 978 0 7022 7037 6 (epdf)

University of Queensland Press uses papers that are natural, renewable and recyclable products made from wood grown in well-managed forests and other controlled sources. The logging and manufacturing processes conform to the environmental regulations of the country of origin.

We who are not there, witnessing from afar,
in what ways are we mutilating ourselves when
we dissociate to cope? To remain human at this
juncture is to remain in agony. Let us remain there:
it is the more honest place from which to speak.

Isabella Hammad

'Who remembers the Armenians?'
I remember them
and I ride the nightmare bus with them
each night

Najwan Darwish

Contents

Introduction

George Abraham

What does it mean to identify oneself with the movement for Palestinian liberation? This is the question running through my mind as I read Omar Sakr's poems, not only for their political clarity, but for the ways they're so unafraid to bridge the distance between Palestinian liberation and the self:

> Some will mutter
> This is not your genocide
> To write poems about
> ...
> I am writing from the trigger
> Of empire.

On one hand, re-reading these words right now, I am brutally reminded of the Arabness that connects us, especially when considering the Zionist entity's* long history of violence against Lebanese, Syrian and other populations in the greater Syria region that we know as Bilad al-Sham. The Zionist entity sees us the same way, as inconvenient at best, as human animal, as the embodiment of imperial disposability and despisability. The pager massacre that murdered several and maimed thousands in Lebanon on 17 September 2024 is but a recent example. Because the world has allowed the Zionist entity to get away with genocide in Gaza, they can and will escalate their colonial violence into the broader region by any means necessary. Countries ago, thinking of the broader history of Bilad al-Sham, the boundaries between us were much more porous, almost non-existent. In the time since, the ghosts of Western, imperially drawn borders haunt us in real time, structuring our mobility and potentials thereof, our economies and potentials thereof, our entire livelihoods. Now, we have come full circle, as the Zionist entity is flattening us all into a dystopian, imperial one-ness.

At the centre of this spiralling catastrophe, there is Palestinian identity, perpetually steadfast, perpetually in *excess of* the reductions of Zionism, imperialism and settler colonialism. Palestinian identity reminds us that, although we are imperially interconnected, Arabness alone has always failed to contain us. The term *Arab* is often weaponised by the Zionist entity to avoid acknowledging *Palestinian* as a category, for instance. Examining the history of Palestine, we also are forced to reckon with the many Indigenous populations (both in Palestine and within the broader South-West Asian and North African region) who are erased by terms like *Arab*. Here, Palestinian-ness forces us to

* This is the translation of an Arabic term for the State of Israel that has a long history.

think harder about the material structures underpinning our identifications. Along these grains, the border between Sakr's speaker and the Palestinians toward whom he writes is one of triggers and empires, of the material structures of our daily realities, instead of a failed neoliberal imagination of identity: one that flattens Arabs without considering the national, economic, racial and material circumstances of our many positionalities—one that has only fetishised, orientalised, barbarised, butchered and disarticulated, at an onto-epistemic level, terms like *Arab* and *Palestinian*.

In many ways, especially considering the past several months of literary organising with accomplices like Omar, we are witnessing the ways in which Palestinian-ness unlocks a mode of insurgent identification that exceeds the boundings, closures and illiteracies of neoliberal identity politics. To identify with Palestinians is not merely a question of blood, land, nation, language or culture; it is inherently a question of material position in the world. It is a reckoning with the excesses of empire, the paradoxes of exile, and the relations necessary to build a more sustainable, life-affirming world free of imperialism, racism and oppression. When, as of late, prestigious literary institutions approach Palestinians with requests to include us in their programming—thus satisfying their needed diversity checkboxes as these very institutions fail to articulate an anti-Zionist politic, let alone a stance that even names our catastrophe a *genocide*—it is unsurprising to see a pattern of Palestinian refusal to participate. The boycott against the Poetry Foundation, one of the most endowed literary institutions in the entire world, was but one example of this, emerging from Omar and myself, alongside Noor Hindi and Summer Farah, collectively refusing to allow our poems in their archives to go viral, again, amid a catastrophe they refuse to acknowledge.

In this way, I have come to understand my own Palestinian-ness as not merely a state of being, but a wholly anti-colonial response/ability and orientation to the world: one that insists on insurgent action responding to ours and every colonial catastrophe—one that insists on hijacking every space I can enter for the service of collective liberation for all of us, pushing the boundaries of neoliberal identity, and forcing us to think beyond it. An identification in the June Jordan 'I was born a Black woman and now I am become a Palestinian' sense, in the Omar Sakr 'I came here for Palestine and found the world' sense, in the insistence on loving Palestinians capaciously, in and beyond one's own poems, knowing nothing less than the whole world is at stake in this fight.

When talking on the phone about this book, Omar told me something that shook me to my core: 'I feel like these are less poems than shadows of poems … I don't have any goals for them besides clarity.' Here, I am reminded of Fargo Nissim Tbakhi's essay 'Notes on Craft: Writing in the Hour of Genocide', which argues that, to wield the page like a weapon, we must replace the imperial machine of Craft—that is, the apparatus that sanitises writing via institutional proximities, neoliberalising influences and the priorities of the state—with the clarity of (insurgent, radical) political theory. At the heart of this collection's reckoning, especially taken alongside Tbakhi's words, is this question of the long cultural Intifada, and more broadly the long middle of our revolutionary movement: how do we keep going, and build the structures to help each other keep going? What role might a poem have in this mobilisation?

At the centre of these inquiries, of course, is the question of what a poem *is*, not understood in some abstract, stakesless, philosophical sense, or some delusional hyperbolic sense that artificially inflates the so-called *power of poetry*, or some strictly utilitarian sense that reduces art to product. No, the vector through which this question is posed is, itself, *us*: the communities these words are reaching toward, the readers (and non-reader actors) implicated in the poems themselves, who, however un/willingly, are likely participants, accomplices and material enablers of Zionist genocide in Gaza if existing as a citizen of a Western country. There is an extraordinary lineage of radical meta-poesis, in and of the Arabic-speaking world, from ancient times to modern poets to contemporary afterlives thereof, carried within the works of poets like Mahmoud Darwish, playwrights like Saadallah Wannous, and interdisciplinary diasporic artists like Fargo Tbakhi, among others. That context is certainly at stake here, but eclipsing any potential invocation of literary lineage is the name that matters most: Gaza. O singular wound. O event horizon to our coming, freer world.

In many ways, *The Nightmare Sequence* is a natural extension of the questions from Sakr's previous collection, *Non-Essential Work*, when refracted through the (gravitational) lens of Gaza specifically. Heavily centred from his last collection's opening section is this exact question of what a poem can offer through a catastrophic grief. Sakr offers a 'Poem after Christchurch', for instance, that is a blank page, followed by a postscript asking: 'What did you imagine there? Write it down… Speak for yourselves, dear monsters. Tell us what you did.' Here, the clarity offered by the poem is one of a mirror: the poem does not want to perform catastrophe or cater to the gaze of a Western audience but, instead, wants to force such a reader to see their own selves in the absenced rubble of us. Here, I am reminded of the recently departed Lebanese writer Elias Khoury, a literal freedom fighter who joined arms and fought to liberate Palestine with the fedayeen, who writes about using literature not to reduce the Nakba into an allegory but, instead, to craft mirrors that force us to see ourselves and each other in catastrophe. Many poems, here and throughout the entirety of Sakr's emerging body of work, join lineage with Khoury, becoming mirrors that clarify as much as they terrify, reminding readers not to be complacent but to join the material fight for a world free of imperialism everywhere.

Another thread I see extended here in *The Nightmare Sequence* is that of catastrophic time. Just as *Non-Essential Work* is deeply embedded into the lived, embodied temporalities of the ongoing global COVID-19 pandemic, *The Nightmare Sequence* asks us to think about what happens to our bodies when suspended within the temporality of Nakba, of genocide, of a world order insistent on an unwavering Zionist alliance. There are, undoubtedly, similarities in the temporal rhythms of life induced by both catastrophes: many Palestinians and our accomplices have felt a sense of abandonment and disillusionment and loneliness, facing desires for 'business as usual' in Western society as our kin in Gaza are being ceaselessly bombed by our countries. We are faced, time and time again, with cycles of willing misinformation, settler-manufactured panic and bad-faith paranoia, and utter lack of accountability from those in power, the net result of which is lives in the order of hundreds of thousands and livelihoods in the order of millions. There's something empowering to see poems that are willing to dissect these phenomena with such clarity; of being told no, in fact, we are not crazy, Palestinians and our accomplices are just being gaslit by a multinational, multibillion-dollar war machine.

As a friend and avid reader of Omar's, I have seen these poems emerging in various contexts, responding moment by moment in these long months since last October. On one hand they are small vessels of clarity, read temporally as Palestinian catastrophe escalates, spirals, loops and winds before our very eyes. With every reprise, we are reminded that, as Lena Khalaf Tuffaha writes, 'Repetition is a Nakba.' One hundred days in, Sakr's poems are no longer themselves but 'a blunt fist' or 'a tear-shaped note to press into a Molotov cocktail or the mouth of an angel'. Some of us never left October 7th, Sakr reminds us, in poems where dates dissolve into centuries, as holidays pass through us like ghosts reminding us, *how the hell are we still in this?* In the temporality of Nakba, echoing with traces of Walter Benjamin's theses,

> History is an angel with seven faces
> All of them are turned away from us.

In this way, these poems are so invested in genocide's assault on living that they exit time altogether; Nakba is not a border in time, but a position we are living in our bodies. These are the abyssal wounds of us: if Gaza is the singularity around which our movement orbits, then Nakba is the event horizon beyond which time and space reverse their coordinates. And like all black holes, catastrophe, too, is inescapable at a molecular level in these poems; Sakr has written a love letter to Palestinians by meeting us here, in the depths of our terrors.

Of the many reasons I am moved by this collection, the parts where I most strongly feel its pulsing heartbeat are when Sakr's speaker is unafraid to confront the ways genocide shapes our most intimate social relations. In poems like 'My wife in the genocide', we are reminded of the particularly devastating inescapability of these atrocities, given the sheer number of children martyred by Zionist genocide, for parents. How can we be married to anything but loss, in this? Sakr writes:

> Every child's corpse is mine, I fear
> Not being able to undo this grim fatherhood,
> I fear its undoing even more.

Here, in the margins and line breaks, these poems live out their nightmares; formally, they operate with the syntactical motions of a shadow breaking against the interruption of daylight, as everywhere in our global community, Arab parents live in the shadow of the impossible lives Gazan parents have had to live every day in this genocide. I say this not to thank these poems for their empathy—for who among us in the West can truly claim to know, at an embodied level, what Palestinian parents have had to endure—but to praise them for their capacious grieving, which holds Palestinians beyond borders such as the un/conscious and the un/knowable. If apocalypse, as Sakr tells us, is a view of death without love, then what these poems give us is the exact opposite: the kind of love that devotes its life force to fighting for beloveds, in mourning. The kind of love that is willing to dive into the depths of one's terrors, into one's own nightmare sequence, to arrive at some other place where we might be more free, or at least more capable of building the kind of liberated world that will never let genocides like this happen again; the kind of love unafraid to 'enter loss from anywhere'. These poems embody the kind of love that holds us in the im/possibility of their images: the miles-long names of our slaughtered, a spoon against the unyielding earth, a silence we dare to name 'the wrong shape'. I want no names for love but this: a love unafraid to meet us in our abyssal wounds, searching for 'the right sequence of sounds that might end the nightmare'.

I have the privilege of having been the recipient of a love poem from Omar: 'Meaning', from his collection *The Lost Arabs*. It ends with the following lines:

> Yaani, do not draw fixed lines around my origin. I came from
> water.
> Yaani, there are waves resonating ever outward. Forget the
> dirt.
> Yaani, meaning Arabs are forever
> transmuting tongue into ocean   to say we are here.

Here, I recall Dionne Brand's lines, 'I do not believe in time, I do believe in water.' They come from her 2022 book-length poem, *Nomenclature for the Time Being*, which ends: 'water doesn't end' (unpunctuated). Brand's words have been echoing in my mind the past several months, especially as I returned to her interview for *Between the Covers*, where she talks about the ways we failed to stop the death machine of the current world order when we had the chance to grind everything to a halt in the COVID-19 pandemic. She spoke of fearing we're spiralling off into our next major catastrophe, and I've felt those words like a prophecy. I am taking Brand and Sakr into the constellation of poets who have, in their words and actions, been integral to my own survival during these times of genocide, alongside Fady Joudah, who gifted us *[...]*, and Lena Khalaf Tuffaha, who wrote *Something About Living* in spectral sisterhood with June Jordan.

Maybe this is the exact kind of love Palestinians are needing from the world right now: a love that moves us beyond acts of witness and into acts of *with*-ness. A love that ends whole worlds because they were built on the backs of ongoing (Black & Indigenous & Palestinian & & &) annihilation. A love that looks at such a world and, instead of offering a balm, offers an ending. A love that does not draw fixed lines. A love that knows when and when not to forget the dirt. A love as unending as water.

George Abraham

THE NIGHTMARE SEQUENCE

Writing poems in the genocide

Some will mutter
This is not your genocide
To write poems about
Not your relatives
Killed and killed and killed—
Thinking being Arab
Or of the ummah means I am writing
From the position of the dead.
Oh habibi, how I wish that were true.
I am writing from the trigger
Of empire. It was not this poem
That paid for the blast, but another.

CRACK!
155K
8,200
28.4K

Sometime in the genocide

It was a Thursday
when thousands of the murdered
passed through me, ungentle
as any love parting.
I ate my dinner on the floor
cold as god, hairy as any animal.
I tried to hold them I think
I reached out at least, shuddering.
They did not slow their passage
and with them went every feeling.

How to identify beloveds in the genocide

By their hands
By the bracelet
By the shape of their absence
In the food line
In the fuel line
By their hands
By the bracelet
By hair peeking out the pile
Do not say they are in pieces
They are everywhere

My wife in the genocide

My phone is awake every hour.
The genocide is across the ocean.
The genocide is in my hand
Splashing lightly on my eyes.
It is too far away to endanger me
But not far enough to escape me
And what my money has nourished.
My wife wants me to be present. How
Do I tell her I am married to loss?
That loss is her wife now, too. Look.
The shadows in our house are red.

Graze in the genocide

My son whose name is radiance
Tripped and skinned
His little knee. My god the wailing!
The wailing in my heart! A blot
Of blood, about the size of the sun
Or my thumb. It was ages ago.
I can still hear it.

Good in the genocide

I have all the records of good
Occurring despite the genocide,
Extravagant kindnesses
The occupied in Gaza managed
To miracle in the misery
From the ______ to the ______
And I will not tell you of them
You do not deserve their beauty

…Look how cruel you've made me.
In whose image was this written?
O God! Forgive me, I still want you
To suffer.

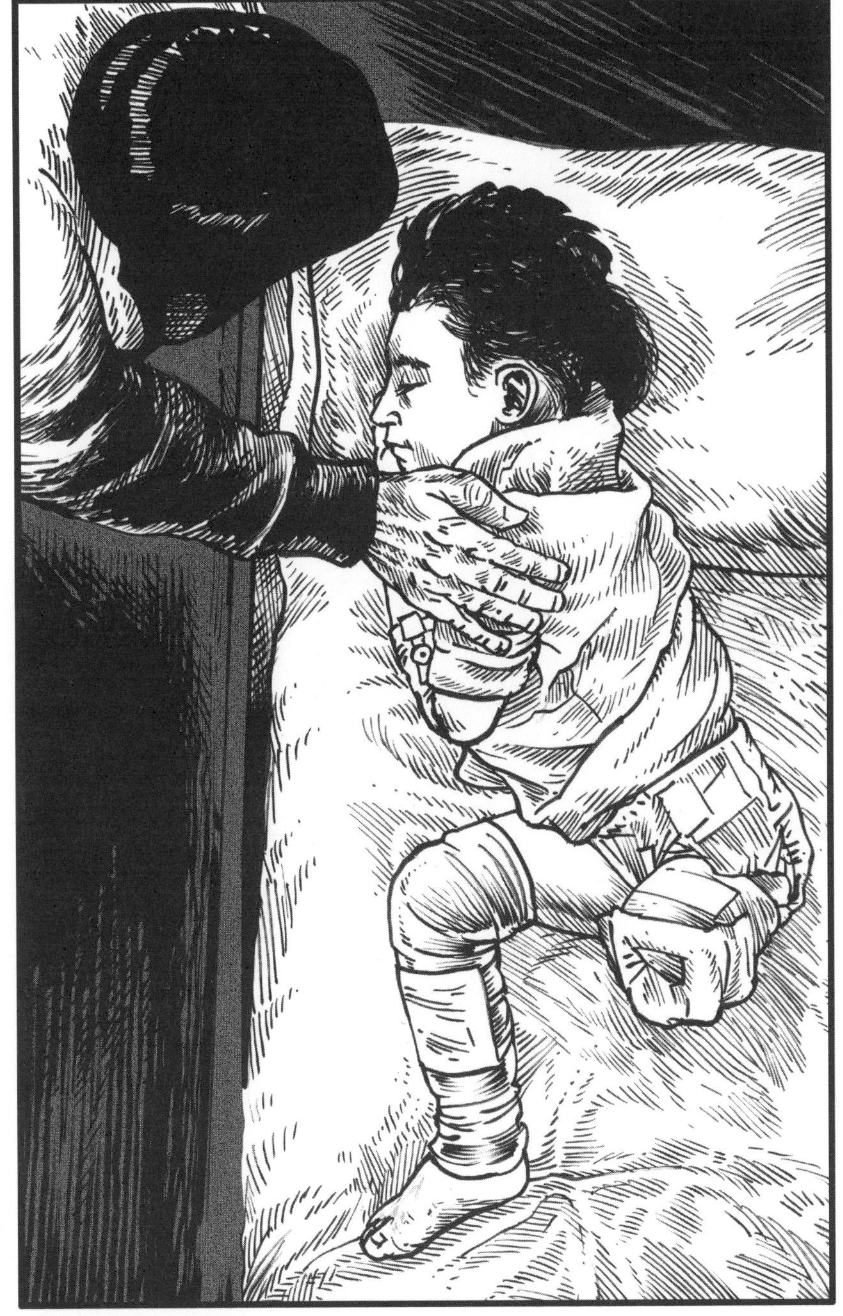

إنتفاضه

Genocide in the genocide

I walk in the fields of genocide
I came here for Palestine
The crowds are enormous, we
Stand shoulder to shoulder, heart
To heart. Here my Yemeni brothers
There my Sudanese sisters;
Here my Rohingya kindred
There my Uyghur beloveds;
Here my Congolese uncles
There my Wiradjuri cousins;
Here my Armenian comrades
There my Kurdish aunties;
Here my Afghan elders
There my Syrian blood;
Here my Iraqi family—
I came here for Palestine and found the world.

If you are searching for yourself, stop.
Everyone is here. The question is:
What are you doing with your hands?

فشلت
الإنسانية

Holocaust in the genocide

The living and dead, my friends
And enemies, all are obscured
By millions of memories—
What some call human
Shields. Nobody has devised
A more complete weapon.

If there were not an Israel, we'd have to invent one.

Legitimacy in the genocide

Elusive as angels before the first bomb
And as common as sky thereafter
Legitimacy proliferates
In the childish eyes of corpses,
Incubators brim with legitimacy
Demolished schools spell out legitimacy
This ugly magic, maker of death!
Soldiers dance on graves legitimately
We are all dying legitimately
And the judges are pleased.

GENOCIDE
CULTURE

Arguing with my sister in the genocide

Is it still true that you refuse to
Believe in jahannam? Her husband
Helpfully adds, think about this:
If a man killed your child
Would you not want him in the inferno?
I said no. They were disappointed.
I should have said something clever
Like, in the dream where my child is killed
I am already in hell and need no company.
Now it is day 27? 15? 31? 22? 68
Of the genocide and I fear that I lied.

فلسطين

Sometime in the genocide (reprise)

Monday, and thousands more
of the murdered pass
ungentle as any love
parting. We have not stopped
the killing; we keep eating.
I hold my child, cold as god.
I try to think. I reach out
At least, shuddering.
Yes, to you. O Mountain!
O River, O Sea! To you &
You & you until we are free
From the winter of our end.

Pause in the genocide

The only one I saw comes in fours, tearing at the unburied dead.

Arab in the genocide

Where are the Arabs where
Are the Arabs they cried

Nobody told them the Arab is dead.
I should know. He was alive in me once—

I saw it happen. I raised the knife.
I left my head on the ground, screaming.

Ya
Rabb
We have
no one
to turn
to but
you!

Masjids in the genocide

Do you imagine I will grieve for one
Piece of rubble more than another?
Do you think there is an inch of land
That isn't holy enough to touch my head
And know God again? Have I not
Told you as endless as death my heart
Is a chorus of prayer? Have you not
Seen us open the door to our murderer
Saying hello brother, over and over?
Do you see my hand on the door now?
Forget what I'm saying, what do you hear?

Rain in the genocide

Drops of relief fall like kids
Into the crater-ponds.
Hands scoop up tainted mai
And all cry out, Thank God!
Thank God! Water, again.
How can you simile bullets
With this? Look at this life!
They are nothing alike.
The ponds run red.
The children are dead.
Never speak to me of rain again.

رحمة

Utility in the genocide

You can't stop this, little poem.
What use is your witness?
Everything is the demand.
All I ask of you is to be
A pillow for Reem
A pillow for Tareq
A pillow for Omar
A pillow for the babies
A pillow for the Babas
A pillow for the mothers
A pillow for the martyrs
And yes, for the fighters.
Softer, softer still.
Rest, beloveds. Rest ya albi.

Tunnels in the genocide

Underground. Subterranean
Subaltern. What lives beneath
The norm, a hollow distance,
A permissive passage, free
Movement. What could be more
Frightening to the prison guard
Than a spoon and unyielding earth
Giving way to the persistent scratch
Of the buried? Nobody could foresee
The day they put the tunnels inside
Each child, an endless expanse
Full of awful possibility, a collapsible
Surface easy to render back into dust.

Air in the genocide

Day after day what I learn distances
Me from the world, and so the world from itself.
In this alienation, nations are alien & violence
Spores in everything. How else
To explain the news reports of air
Continually striking children and families
Dead? 'Air strikes—' 'Air strikes—' 'Air strikes—'
What have we done to turn breath against us?
Oh, death has always been invisible I know
God's lovely hand, but murder? Murder is
Human: a face, a name, hair, eyes, grin.
Like you, I have smashed every mirror.
Like you, I cannot escape the air.

In London during 'The Blitz' (1941) the German Luftwaffe dropped 711 tonnes of explosives.

In Hamburg (1943) the Allies dropped 2326 tonnes.

In Hiroshima (1945) the Americans dropped an atomic weapon the equivalent of 16,000 tonnes.

In Gaza (2023-24) Israel has dropped over 85,000 tonnes and counting.

GENOCIDE
CULTURE
Sarafand
al-Amr
1918

Bluey in the genocide

We watch the cricket episode,
All laconic drawls and summer
Games, a dedicated pup learning
To play while his father is away.
His name is Rusty, he's a star
At bat. My son laps it up, as do I
Until the end; the scene shifts
And there is the distant dad
In combat fatigues, and I learn
Even in this cartoon world
There is a desert full of dogs
Soldiers and guns, and somewhere
Out of frame, Arabs being put down.

His name is Mansour. Whenever he's with me I feel safe.
If I live my bird will live with me.

Reflection in the genocide

My son alights on his prize—a mirrored box—and is transfigured. He can see himself and wants nothing more than to release what's within. He shakes his arm, producing a rhythmic clatter. He can't get in. He can't let go. He careens around the living, his whole body bent to the task, distracted by the music made in the struggle. I've seen this process play out with a flower, a book, a banana, the moon, the wind; he is always clutching something. My hands are full of loss. I can't get in. I can't let go.

Kisses in the genocide

I used to tear out clumps of hair
Fistfuls of white and grey, stark
Against the black. Until the day
Ato told me each brilliant fleck
Marked the kiss of an ancestor. Now
When I look in the mirror I'm swept
Under the silver field, the early elders
The astonishing weight of love.

Looking away in the genocide

I have, too many times to count.
There's no anaesthetic left.
Do you understand? Nothing
To blunt the pain. I'm no hero,
This isn't brave, it's a blank page
My pen, and blood. In my chest
I have a stadium of dead children
I swear it's full yet every day
Another is added. It isn't the dead
I look away from, it's the debt
Owed the living, dragging down
My eyelids, turning stay into flee
Turning love into solidarity
Something bearable, distant, a politic.
I'm trying to see and not scream.
Therein lies the problem.

Comprehension in the genocide

My son's speech is delayed, they say
His ears rush with fluid, his mouth
Torrents a river divine, iggy bidgy
Shush book ha Baba! I gibber back
At him, I repeat myself, myself
Repeats: can you say… the question
A hook—the bait, my love.
Why does this feel so cruel?
To want to hear my name
Alive in him. The metaphor
Won't release the line. It breaks!
I understand nothing. Nothing
Understands me. Tah lehon
Ya ibni. Spit by spit, here is
The gleaming a life hangs on,
The reel spun into night
To catch on a piece of world
Anything other than a body—
A sodden tyre or boot, words,
A refrain, yaani, signs of use.

Why does this feel so cruel?
I'm caught, by God! Unfasten me!
Why is every question a hook?
What will it take for you to love me?
When the answer wriggles, alive
In your hands, will you eat it
Or let it go free

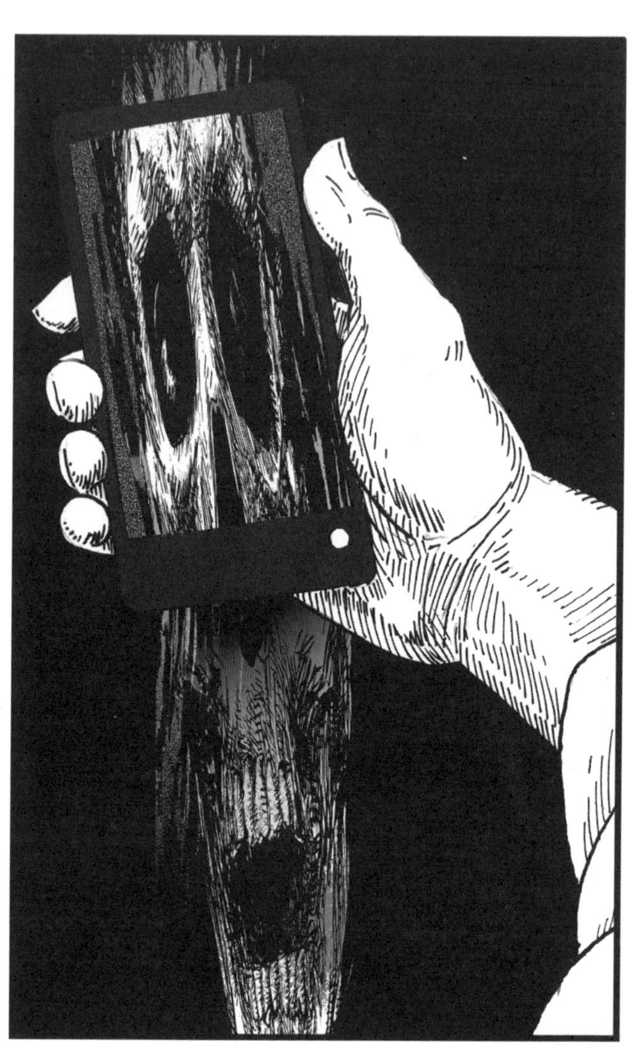

Clicks in the genocide

All the images come veiled.
The madmen's gauze above Gaza,
An algorithm's dream of safety.
Even the sky has a burial shroud
While killers grin at the cameras.
Which of us should be covered?
I know what a veil means. To bare
Witness can be an act of love or
Violence. Click here to make
Your choice. We're family now
& I wouldn't wish that on anyone.

alt txt in the genocide

Image description #1:
The warm hand of the father
The warm hand of the daughter
Together clasp the cold son.

Image description #2:
Please
Don't make me write
Another
I beg you
How many hauntings
Must we bear

Working in the genocide

Necessity is the darkest mask
And it fits no one perfectly.
I want this day to go differently.
I could plant a seed.
I could sing a song.
I could leave the building the bank calls home.
I could make the earth my solace.
I could live off the land—OK, maybe not, but
I could try. Even unwashed, even dead
I would be cleaner and more alive.
Instead, I go to work in the genocide
And write odes to failure on my lunch break.
Today necessity speaks with my son's face,
Asking, Baba, how did you answer the times?

Say in the genocide

Say this has no purpose.
Say no one reads it.
Am I not alive to myself?
Say it is meaningful.
Say everyone reads it.
More, say it's understood.
Now we're talking.
Say my feeling meets yours
And together they deepen,
Is that enough? Are we better
For it or at risk of drowning?
Either way, I'm not calling
Out to be saved. Keep me
Away from the shore. Take
My voice into a dark room.
Get rough if you must, we are
Alone. Say the screams are yours.
Say your next life is in Gaza.
Say my last life was in Gaza.
Say we will all wake there tomorrow
In the genocide, who would sleep tonight?

GENOCIDE
CULTURE

I've had enough...

Grief in the genocide

Not an hour passes without a murder
Brought to my artless hands and heart.
Before the poem, I am breathless.
Before the poem, I kiss the beards
Of the dead. Before the poem I argue
A thousand and one times with God
In the court of despair, and lose.
Before I come to you like this
I gift a million verses to the moon
Telling her to recite them to Falastin.
Who knows if she listens? Who knows
If Gaza hears her speaking soft as milk?
I am here with my stupid pen regardless
Still grieving 1948, still pressing my lips
Against Abel's cheek.

Demonstrations in the genocide

Show, don't tell the imagists say,
After a lifetime ignoring our voices.
Perform for us, Charlie. Here is a public
Square full of ten thousand shoes.
Kid-sized. All your favourite brands.
Nike, Reebok, Adidas. Lesser-knowns
& knock-offs too. Look at these ghosts.
Look at this silence, it has a shape
And more than ten thousand names.
I understand the impulse, it echoes
History, and literature, but Hemingway's
Six words are no longer universal.
Nobody cares for an Arab's shoes,
Nor the bodies they belonged to.
Look at them all piling up to heaven
And still the killing hasn't stopped.
Silence is the wrong shape for this,
Don't you know? Absence synonyms
Arab already. Silence is the wrong shape.
I have only one child and every hour
He shatters my eardrums.

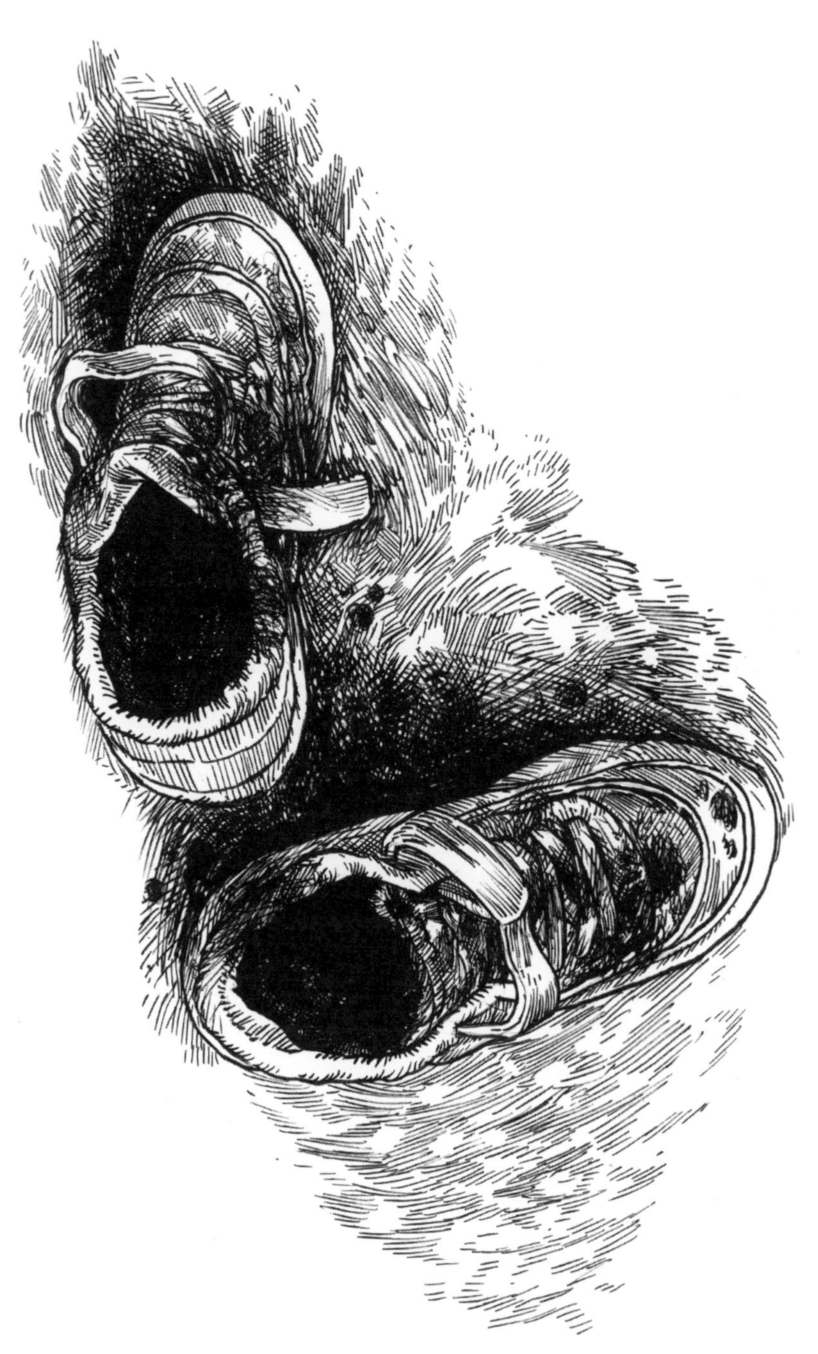

GENOCIDE
CULTURE

100 days in the genocide

I don't have a poem for this.
Everything I write in the genocide
        Is the shadow of a real
Poem: a blunt fist, a stern shake, a tear
-Shaped note to press into
        A Molotov cocktail
Or the mouth of an angel.

Dates in the genocide

The date is drummed into your teeth.
The date is packed in 30 000 munitions.
The date drains the water pipes, blisters
Every child's throat. The date cluster
Bombs hospitals, the date assassinates
Doctors, the date drones above the sleepless,
The date strips fathers on the street
The date burns through skin and bones.
Nobody is responsible for anything now.
A date cannot be arrested, nor stopped—
We know this thanks to the Americans—
A date is the perfect forever killer, abstract

Reaper. We don't have a date to stamp
On your face: we have centuries.

GENOCIDE
CULTURE

October 7th in the genocide

You think I fear to enter October 7th?
Habibi, I never left. I'm still there with you

Dying as I do every day. I admit I can't see
the murdered you heap murder on.

Which of us disgraces them more, do you think?
Ten thousand children want to know.

You think the world didn't break that day
For me the world breaks every day.

You think the heart's task isn't remaking loss.
You think I won't write of your loves,

When the real danger is that I will. Relax,
My hands are cramped around a million epitaphs.

It will take me roughly all the time in the world
To get there. You think my poetry is a weapon.

And it is. Each line is my fist striking your chest,
Each stanza is my ear pressed against it, hoping

To hear a single beat.

GENOCIDE
CULTURE
Sderot Cinema

Unloved in the genocide

Those who mourn the fall of a prison wall
Think my eyes are closed.

The guards were people,
Too, they say, look how much we loved them—

Count everyone we kill, laughing, in their names—
Have you ever seen such love? Bereft,

I tell them no. Description falters, gallops
In the other direction. What's the old saying?

Something about a horse and water
The steaming flanks on the bank

Giving way in the heat, parched and unable
To take in anything but itself.

Hope in the genocide

Every night I read to my son a story called *Hope.*
It's about a boy, Finn, and his sick dog.
Finn's father gives him a flashlight.
He demonstrates how to burn a hole in the night.
This is his metaphor for hope: the action
Of keeping a little light on in the dark
My son now knows the word 'hope' though
In his unfilled mouth it emerges as hop—
Maybe that's a better metaphor for it—a leap
Moving us across a lack, but anyway, tonight
I learned how sounds and meaning diverge.
My son pointed at Finn and said hope.
He did not point at the light. He understood
The story better than I. He knew what must be
Preserved, but not yet how much has already been
Extinguished, how many skies emptied of sons.

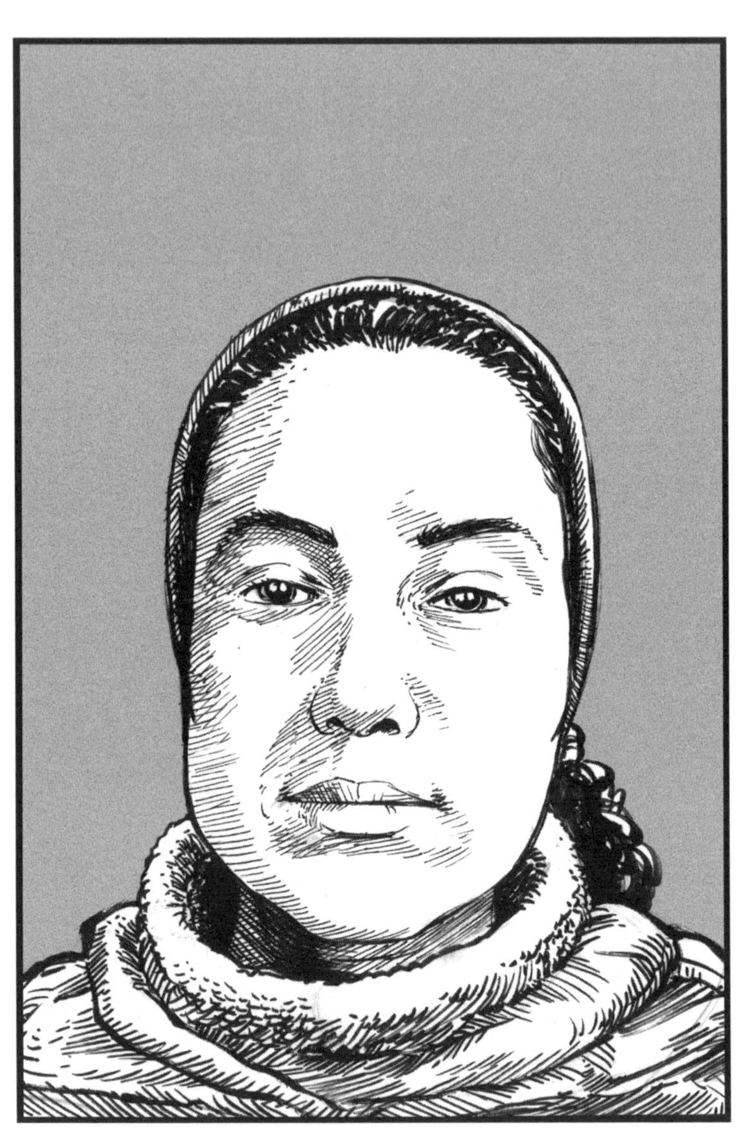

Witness in the genocide

Being seen is anathema to an oppressor
Though they preen in every mirror
What delights is a mirage. I promise you
The deathmakers are rigorous in their unsight,
They take out any eye that sees them—
Bullets for the reporter, bullets for the camera
And the cornea, a smothering of power
A smearing of voices that name them true.
Pity the devil this pointless violence, this ruin
Of every witness. You are never alone
On this earth. O murderer of this life
You have forgotten the ant and the bee,
You have forgotten the rain and the leaf,
You have forgotten the winged and the wind,
You have forgotten yourself. Oh, being
Seen is anathema to an oppressor, for knowledge
Is the surest path to love, which they disown.
Did you know that love is ours from the outset,
Like breath, unconscious and unconditional,
That you must learn how to *not*? Back there,
Somewhere on your road, you stopped breathing
And I promise you, there was a witness.

Algo in the genocide

Okay I won't use the word *Jewish*
And I won't use the word *Zionist*
And I won't use the word *genocide*
And I won't use the word *apartheid*
And I won't use the word *settler*
And I won't use the word *colony*
And I won't use the word *killed*
And I won't use the word *watermelon*
And I won't use the word *Palestine*
And I won't use the word *resistance*
And I won't use the word *law*
And I won't use the word *moral*
And I won't use the word *men*
And I won't use the word *God*
And I won't use the word *river*
And I won't use the word *sea*
And I won't use the word *free*
And I won't use the word *children*
For the young of _____ are always _____
What are we left with at the end?
A murdered dictionary and field
After silent field of unmarked graves.

GENOCIDE
CULTURE

Elegy in the genocide

Only now, facing the outer limits,
Do I understand myself as capable
Of lending grace to matter, having
Done so before, in at least one poem.
I was a miracle-maker, dear reader
And so were you—I could witness a rot
Or flower, a divorce, a dress, a broom
Any little thing, and fill it with God. Once
We could do such things, and now?
Not. We live here now. In the not.
In revolting clay unable to reflect
Even the dimmest light of dead stars.
I've seen too many murdered children
I failed to save. This is a salve for no one
A signal to an abandoned station,
Not poetry so much as muscle memory
For the spirit departed. I live in the not.
The not-me. The not-world. The not-heart
And not-society. And still the dead heap
In my eyes, and still I weep, and still my body
Carries on its minute motions. If I could
Dear martyr, I would not leave you here
In a poem, but in my arms—I would gather you,
Each red part, into a white cloth, I would
Clean you and prepare you for the earth
Our mother, with a kiss for each wound,
Until we once more resemble people.

Valentine in the genocide

The Romans executed Valentine.
In February, they danced naked, drunk.
They sacrificed animals and beat women
And fucked in a glut. The Christians
Replaced the day with their own.
The Romans executed Valentine
And the martyr became a saint.
It was that easy. In Gaza, saints
Multiply faster than anywhere else
On Earth. In Palestine, where Isa wept,
Love is survival, and new names shake
The breath of angels: Hind, Sidra, Malek.

Names in the genocide

Much is made of the names of the dead
Especially the youngest, as if one can age
Into a better murder. I mourn
My teyta still, years later, babbanne too.
What can a name do absent love? What
Does it mean next to missiles signed
With a flourish, one name ending
Hundreds, happily. I don't know
What to call myself anymore. I
Watched the videos listing the killed
I'm told to print them all here
Would make this poem miles long
& I don't want that. Either you can hold it
In your hands or else it must stretch
To cover the Earth.

صمود

Limits in the genocide

Every child's corpse is mine, I fear
Not being able to undo this grim fatherhood,
I fear its undoing even more. Since the birth
Of my son, I see him everywhere, dying
And living and starving, babushka boy
Buried thirteen thousand times at least
And I'm not inured, much as I beg to be,
To the ruins arriving with each dawn
And shroud. Of course I've gone mad,
What else could you expect? Who
Would choose to father this world,
Every single child, voluntarily?
Don't tell me that's what we did.
God knows I'm not God—I'm just
Looking for the limits everyone testifies
A heart must have, an intangible
Fatigue. A line where care stops.
Where is the line that stops care?
I haven't found it, God. Come closer
If you have, love. Whisper the words
In my ear. I will take them to my grave.

AMBUL
02
CIVIL DEFENCE

Passer-by in the genocide

I'm sitting with Fahad under a tree
When a passer-by leans in close
'You're not going to stop the war
Sitting there,' he whispers, like a prayer,
A hoped-for thing, among other wicked
Fictions like 'I wish you the best.'
I don't speak. Wait for him to leave.
Wish we had ahwii to scald the tongue
As much as the sun. We have water
At least, the air, the tree with its names
And faces, green canopy of loss.
A passer-by could never understand.
We're not here for you, nor the minister.
We're here for our brothers and sisters
They are right above us, lifted by every
Breath, fingers trailing in our hair.
Keep walking, dear passer-by.
Even alone we are never alone.

Refusal in the genocide

For Aaron Bushnell

He walked to the gate
Accelerant in hand.
I can't make this beautiful
I hope you understand.
His voice was clear.
He tried to ignite
The spark of his life
Several times.
I'm stuck on his fingers
On the catch
On the flash
On the free
On Falastin
Screaming
I don't need a poem
I need a fire extinguisher

But oh god
Nothing can quench this light.

الإحتلال يولد المقاومة

Please don't scroll! I need just a few seconds of your time...
506
52

Timely in the genocide

In the Arabic after Marwa Helal

dearest, time in I Am
out step I Can
death arrest To
Verse a With
matrix as Metre
face we do Or
ourselves Only
Please? Page this On
for time in I am who me Tell
here always am I it is How
limelight killing In
birth ancestors my Before

POLIZEI
BE
D1312
POLIZEI
BE
D1313
POLIZE
BE
D1310

History in the genocide

Oh yes, our oldest mother is loved.
She is invoked each hour.
She lies heavy on every tongue.
She covers millions of eyes.
One day! One day! One day
They say, someone will care
Enough. They say, this will be
Recorded. You'll see, won't you?
History is an angel with seven faces
All of them are turned away from us.

Park in the genocide

Any dark man with a beard
Could be me I have learned
From my son's urgent delight
How he rushes to love them.
Dear fathers afraid to smile
Do you know he is yours, too?
He doesn't know you
Could be a danger and I
Fear to teach him where joy
Must be tempered. In my youth
I ran from everyone, everywhere,
With good reason. What reason
Holds you at bay, dear fathers?
Is it a memory or a fear,
Is it yours or was it given,
Is there a difference, Baba?
I look around at the sum of us
And count all the flinches.

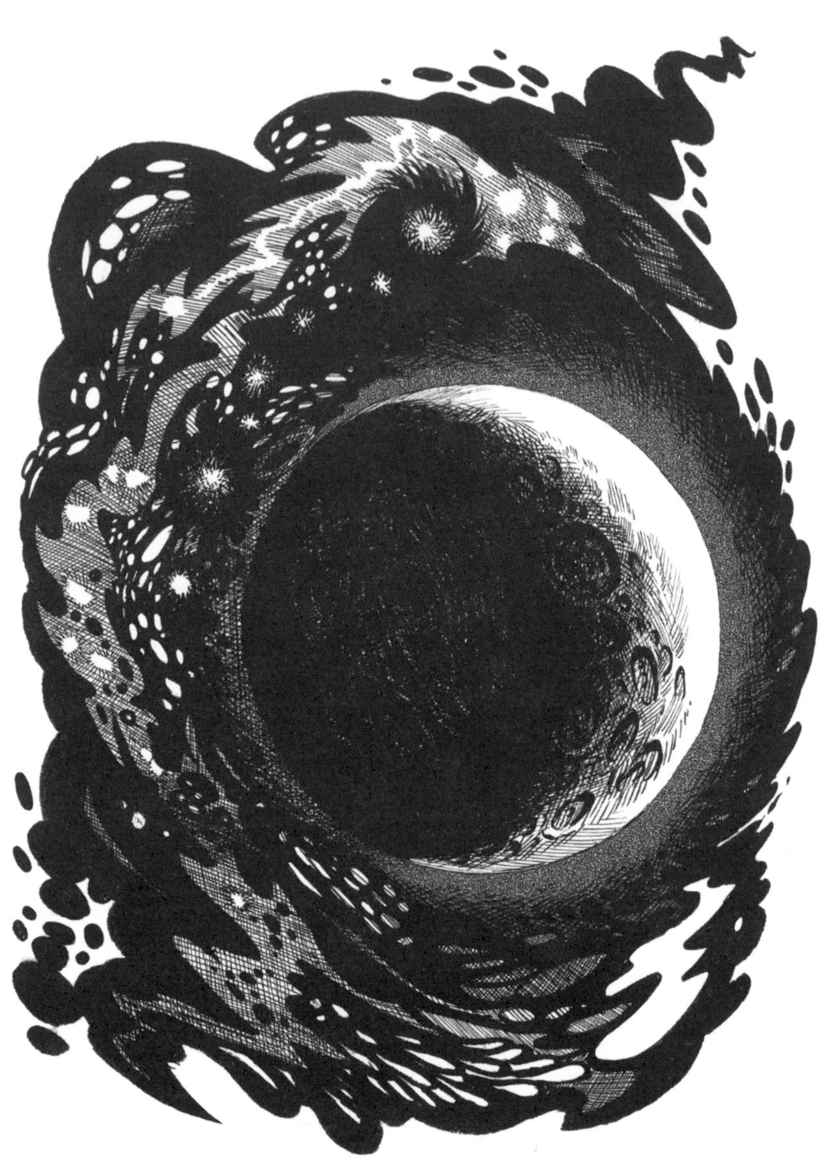

Ramadan in the genocide (I)

The moon begins again.
Becomes visible, I mean,
The edge. I rise in the dark
To test my hunger, how holy
I can be if given a chance,
A parameter, a limit
To reach and retreat.
I am to position myself
Growl to growl, pang
To pang, near those with less
As if we who have more
Did not take it from their hands.
Look how empathy eats itself.
Ya Allah I can already taste
How we break.

Ramadan in the genocide (II)

How do you *go without*
Without something
To subtract from?
O, nobody has nothing!
There is always history
And love, for example—
Which will you give up
For the span of sunlight
To show your fortitude?
I am not strong enough
God, to last even an hour.

Product placement in the genocide

The blare of the Coke lid, the black shine held by hostage glass.
The Disney backpack next to the once-child quartered into forever.
The gold McDonald smile scrunched under combat boots.
These obvious obscenities you'd cringe at in the cinema.
It's not a spectacle—it's life, ours, theirs—yet we watch,
Do we not? And rarely act as anything other than background.
Who designed this set? Why couldn't you hide our money better?
I need money to live! Money said so! I don't want to be killed
Or left alone to die in a king's dungeon. I hear this often
In the shadow of projections. Oh it's true that money needs us.
To make a king. To build a dungeon, and gild hungry gods.
Future tense, yes. They are here and never finished arriving.
Don't tell me to be subtle now, it's too late for that.
I have a child's intestines stuffed inside my wallet.
What are you buying with this blood, this leather? Everything
Is for sale, every wood and river, every life and death.
As the credits roll, we wake as people in the dark
Coins spent like any childhood. No hope for a refund.

Recycling in the genocide

They ran out of regular death and had to resort to using some old junk death commissioned for the Korean War; for other Other bodies, to induce Other screams and Other flames, to eat Other childhoods. How precise do the labels need to be on the murder machines? How precise do the labels need to be on the hands that use them? They say Israelis cried out in Hebrew 'I am you!' and were still killed by other Israelis. Such dedication! Death has never had more diligent disciples. No I don't want to write another word but how can I do less? I will manufacture another line! God as my witness these poems will break the sound barrier! They will bloom the night! They will tear away the veil of life! And you will not see the poem coming which steals away your breath.

Easter in the genocide

Days of betrayal precede us.
Shops have finally closed their doors
Not to the current murderers
In the Holy Land, but to remember
Ancient acts of atrocity &
Renewal. Is this atonement?
What did you give up this Lent?
Here come the last days of Ramadan.
Together we watch Palestinians starve
To death as if they might rise again.
Can you imagine the sacrilege
Of calling any of these days holy?
One of these nights will be full of angels.
One of these nights the night will break
And heaven will hear us. I have searched
For the right words all my life. Discarded
Curse after curse and I will not ask
For what we do not deserve. I can
See the Night ahead, the rush of wings.
I will let it pass. This is for you, reader:
When did you tender your resignation
To grace? When did you give it all up
To after? You could earn a grain of it
I swear, if only you worked up a sweat
To save anyone other than yourself.

و لنا عودةٔ

FUTILITY

200 days in the genocide

I poem this.
Everything in the genocide
        Is the shadow of a real
Me: a blunt tear
        In the mouth of an angel.

What matters about Palestine is what has always prevented Israel from converting its military superiority into lasting political gains: that invincible Palestinian desire to keep hold of what is right and to reject what is wrong.

Angles that didn't work in the genocide

Think of the children. *Think youngest.*
Think of the women. *Think pregnant.*
Think of the incubators. *Think powerless.*
Think of the (gentle) men. *Think old.*
Think of the disabled. *Think amputated.*
Think of the queers. *Think rejected.*
Think of the animals. *Think human.*
Think of the Christians. *Think white.*
Think of the heritage buildings. *Think once.*
Think of the future past. *Think now.*
Think of the universities. *Think tank.*
Think of the environment. *Think residue.*
Think of the hospitals. *Think investment.*
Think of the doctors. *Think cutting.*
Think of the nurses. *Think maternal.*
Think of the diseases. *Think PPE.*
Think of the journalists. *Think trial.*
Think of the UN employees. *Think borders.*
Think of the starving masses. *Think bone.*
Think of the geopolitical. *Think revolution.*
Think of the buried alive. *Think safe.*
Think what comes after hell. *Think you*
Of the spaces between thought—*think country*
And deed, of all we used to affirm—*think fantasy*—
Warranted protection from harm. *Think absence.*
Who are the acceptable targets? *Think darker.*
The ones we don't have to mention. *Think Muslim.*
At the beginning of every ending, think Palestinian.

Mother's Day in the genocide

Arab women love to tell their children the Prophet, peace be
Upon him, said that the way to heaven lies at your mother's feet.
As in, devotion begins there. As in, there are six thousand ways
To heaven buried in Gaza; as in, every road to God lies in a mass grave;
As in, there are nineteen thousand children wandering in circles; as in
All the lines are crossed; as in, I shouldn't take sacred injunctions
This literally; as in, my religion is autistic; as in, I keep rebounding
From words; as in, we should define *mother*; as in, the toll is higher
Than you imagine; as in, I mothered so hard today my son snapped;
As in, the ways to Jannah are incalculable; as in, who has the time
To count that many toes; as in, get on the damn floor; as in, each tear
Mothers an angel, yaani, we have all of us birthed a celestial host;
As in, why aren't you weeping yet, you fool, these waters are godly;
As in, ya immi, thank you for these eyes, this ache, my endless love.

The Nightmare Sequence

Mute, I face my mother, need to unmet need,
time's violence paused while I search for the right
sequence of sounds that might end the nightmare,
stop what I know comes next. What I know comes next
now at my behest and this is sometimes the difference
between life and death. My sweetest delusion
flowers—that I can edge this dread or escape myself,
unlock my body from my body and this place—
if only I immerse myself in the paradise hues
of the bruise, the delicate brushstrokes, then
the blow will not be felt. Instead, I become
the agent of my oldest pain, I replace her,
I make music of us, I distract and detract
because the nightmare learns, the dark adapts.

The nightmare learns, the dark adapts.
I play at language again, plucking every chord
to find the door that will release my trapped
breath. This is not a meditation for what was,
this is an emergency intervention, sirens
careening to bring paramedics to a man
who never gets off the line because the line once
kept his body alive, the line pierced his throat,
whistled blood whistled *wait, help is coming.*
Having worked once before is enough to justify
an eternity of trying; I say this of love and poems,
why not the world? Why not the twisted dream
locking land and people in a death grip? Must I
dream smaller, Lord? Is anything beneath you?

Beneath anything is a dream of you, Lord.
I return to your first command, *read*,
which secrets another: *write*. When I can
do neither, I am the furthest from holiness.
In the unreadable face of genocide, Ya Rab,
I'm looking at myself squatting in murder,
trying to sleep in the reek and becoming,
slowly, my mother, demented
by what I'm told to bear with grace.
Where is the sequence of sound for this,
the syntax sublime that can unravel hate
or gum up the gun factories? I mean
stun them with a strike, a local, global strike,
until all the bullet-makers lie stricken!

Until all the bullet-makers lie stricken
and incapable, I will keep my poems armed
with meaning to render the heart alive—O strike!
That sound invokes the missile, the raised hand
not the removed one, not the refusal to harm.
Can the absence of work be so devastating?
Will it crater the earth? Who cowers now
at the whistle of this word, this strike? Go ahead
and choose your meaning; this is a small enough
dream for you, to live in the margin of error.
Fear not, I have enough fear for all of us,
enough shame for all of us, to think I've spent decades
on this dirt without making a devil wake in fright,
or letting the child in me finally speak.

Let the child in me finally speak: mother, my first devil,
I'm not your wound, I'm not you at all, not him,
not that moment, not redemption, not disgrace,
not history come alive to taunt you with yourself,
not a body or person you've come across before.
Stay with this: I am a stranger you
have never met, and if you understood this,
I would be unbruised today. I survey
my children, these gorgeous helpless others,
and listen as each person quarters their bodies—
'They have your eyes but her lips but your nose
but his knees but your jido's ears but—'
the babies are fundamentally themselves,
perfect and fragile as a memory of morning dew.

Mourning is memory's due, transforming in light.
Each day I face a stranger child and reintroduce myself
and the world; the sun, the night, the cup, the colours,
the limits, the love, and hope they, my beloved
captives will bear my presence with less than terror
and come to know me not just as food or shelter,
not just as song before sleep or Baba, nor as implacable
keeper of the sharpest edges, reluctant world-namer,
but as a man reducible to seed, to once, to dirt, to mother;
there she is again. The figure, not the person,
who I still have yet to see, or place here—wherever
we are real, it is not in the past—O how I love the figure
and not mum herself! How I love to blame others
for my faults! We are each of us alone in our history.

For my faults, we are each of us alone in our history.
Fleeing the figure of love, I haunt myself in advance of death,
there's no mothering to be found in the hollow of my chest,
only muttering, only hissed imprecations and devoted flagellations—
look, oh look! How I arrive to you pre-judged
so as not to face rejection. Yaani, I reject myself, God!
I want for this to be true more than anything,
but I fear these are tortured echoes of my mother's mind
and together, we refuse to open, to turn toward each other,
to dare, to say here is one unmarred stretch of tender skin
you can strike if you want… or hold, softly, or press lips to in apology.
Find me an unmarred stretch of tender skin, would you
risk again the hubris of love, or what we ape as such.
There is a genocide here—give up speaking of love!

Speaking of love, the genocide is here—only you
refuse to see it. I keep telling you I'm not there.
I keep telling you I'm burrowed in empire's heart,
radioactive to the cancer, poison fighting poison yes,
gorged on rot; I keep telling you the genocide began
before I was born, and with each strike of these keys
another child is murdered, another head bursts,
another angel shrieks in the void of heaven;
I keep telling you we are the same and still
you return me to the rubble, still you receive me
in the massacre of myself, the one figure you won't let go of
O Arab, killable, erasable spirit, coloniser and colonised,
ancient colossus, agent of unreason, fat grape
for Earth's stamping feet. Drink, darling, drink.

I'm drunk on this stomping, darling Earth. Why
shouldn't we miracle the grimace as well as the smile,
the shit as well as the wine? Pour another one
and I'll tell you these final secrets, knowing
you will not retain them, and we'll return here
under the moon's eye, naked and foolish:
I cannot make my people more alive to you.
The word victim is as much a trap as any act.
There are narcissists in the extermination camp, too.
Will you love them less? Show me a child
not in love with themselves and the world, I dare you.
There are mothers and sons locked in memories, unable
to speak to each other, even without missiles; there are
fathers clouded with dust, left with nothing but poems.

O father clouded with poems, bring your dusty brow
to these lips! I'm here, in the annihilation of love.
Does that comfort you? It does nothing for me.
I'm holding my children, their every agony,
I'm holding my blessings like a shield against
the world's cruel meaninglessness, and one
or the other must rupture but I'll be damned if it's us.
Reader, you will not like this, but dawn is closing in,
and we must part with the truth: when I told you
that we are in hell, even those who nodded along
imagined themselves therein as misplaced observers,
casual Dantes taking a gander, temporarily embarrassed
angels. There's no road out of this, no forthcoming divine
comedy and I'm sorry, so sorry, I can't stop laughing.

FROM THE RIVER
TO THE SEA
PALESTINE
WILL
BE
FREE!
BOYCOTT
ISRAEL
BDS
JEWS FOR
A FREE
PALESTINE
NO JUSTICE
NO PEACE
END THE
OCCUPATION!

Protest in the genocide

How will I get you, my loneliest eye, to love
Another? Oh, let me define it for you then,
The precise process of divine arrival—
It's not so much a fall as it is an expulsion
Out of self, into the ache of world
Where even a breath can flay
Your spirit, yet you inhale anyway
To know the air between us,
How much more alive we can be
When we breathe together. Love is both
The path toward devastation, and the means
By which we survive it. What are you
Waiting for? Leap! You are alone in yourself!
Leap! There is more to this life! Even to death
Yes, leap! For your husband and your wife
For your friend and your child, for the river
And the sea, for the stranger you can't see
And the day you might not meet—leap!

Father's Day in the genocide

People love the poems about my mother,
About mothers, about women and their children.
I know why. Even when my mother wields a blade in a verse,
We remember to ask, who gave her the blade?
Who showed her how to swing? How to sharpen
Her voice to a point? How to beat the body black?
Who redefined for her what is tolerable?
She is no innovator, I tell you.
What of the father behind the father? How far
Back in time must you go to land at a kind life or loving
Finale? According to the Prophet, peace be upon him,
Fathers form the middle of your gate to paradise.
Since mine was absent in life, my gate is not a gate at all
But an arch through which all the winds can travel.
Baba! I still love you, O broken door! Ana Abu Nayirr.
My son, you who changed my name, know this please:
Whenever I should hurt you, I am the only one to blame
And it will fall on me to mourn ever having marred heaven.

Small talk in the genocide

Where are you going? Avoiding the obvious, the impossible.

I can hear the wind. Smell the rain.

Did you sleep? Mashallah.

My son is crying, sorry, give me a minute. Imagine that.
The wonder of a minute.

Did you see—? God. Oh god!

I know, I know. I've never felt smaller. Or larger.

Prayer is like that. Bigger on the inside.

Hold on, I have to change his nappy.

Please, I could weep with happiness at the filth of his living.

How is work? How can you work? I'm working at it.

I've never seen silence take over so much. A whole horizon,
full and bristling.

Look around: everyone is running in place.

Yes, I'll meet you anywhere we can scream with purpose.

Have you eaten? Ramadan is over but I still hesitate before opening my mouth.

Here is the power of permission: when withdrawn, it haunts the once-blessed vessel.

Yaani starve once, you starve forever. It's on me, it's in me, every wound, forever.

He's teething, yeah. I'm trying to love his wailing, because.

Comparison demands such unholy alchemy.

My problem with globalisation is I have too many untouchable loves now.

This is killing me.

Nothing is harder 'in this moment'. This isn't a moment, it's a habit

Decades in the making, a forever wound no one can swallow, a jawbreaker.

I don't know what an unbroken jaw looks like, my ancestors' mouths gape open.

Honestly, I'm so relieved to have a love larger than myself,
here in my home

I can't accept words like hard or struggle, he is my divine
question mark

My delirious answer to everything, even the untold sorrows.

Hold the line, will you? I just want to hear you breathe.

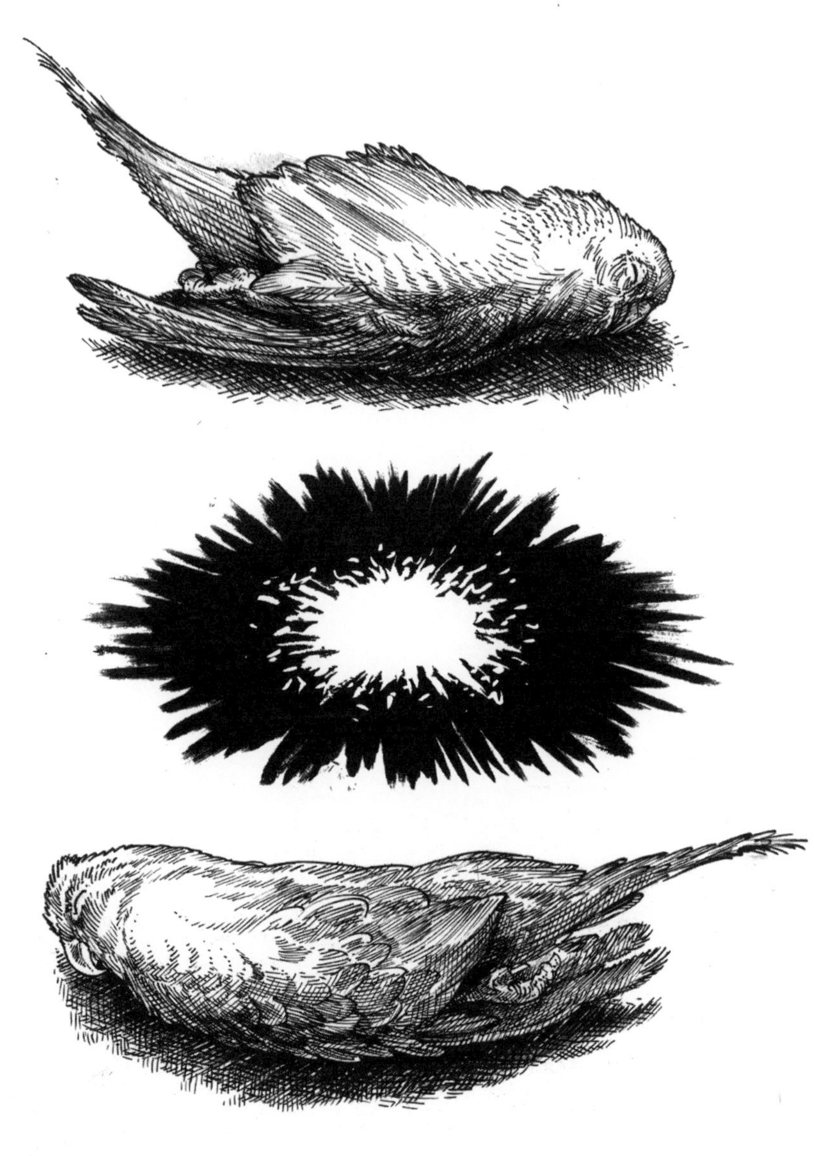

Israel's pager attack in Lebanon killed 9 people, including an 8-year-old girl. 2800 people were wounded, 200 of them critically.
BRRRRRRRRR
01
15:30
17/09/24
CRACK

Australian media responded with applause.
005 TPIP U
It was an audacious 'James Bond-style' attack…
Like something from a spy movie!

PRESS

Words in the genocide

There are no words for this, we repeat.
I think about this instead of the dead.
The brain matter. The reddened kids.
There have never been more words.
In English, and Arabic: a thousand
novels, a hundred thousand poems,
decades of song, laws days-long,
a thesis stack that can reach the sun.
What if I told you the reader is moved
not at all? The listener laughs, stuffed
in a mangled woman's wedding dress.
No doubt the Times would edit her out—
the original woman, the marriage, flesh.
Murderers wear their victims' clothes
in demolished homes, grinning;
I can't think of a better description
for Zionism. Killing my love of drag
is the least of its crimes. I think
about the seamstresses, and tailors.
The careful measurements,
months of labour, the elegance
of knuckles, an art meant to be
recorded from every angle to stun
even the future. How they worked
their whole lives to be in the picture.
How we work just as hard not to be.
Like the times, I edit us out of frame.

Social cohesion in the genocide

The egg, big as a baby's head, falls
And all the king's horses, all his men
Come together to fail in unison.
In this story, the egg is brown
And full of untranslatable life.
In this story, a doddering king
Pushes the egg over the edge
Again and again. Who doesn't
Love a crisis? He watches
The theatre below, the actors
Rushing to staunch the loss,
Stitch the unsolvable wound,
To rage, and inevitably, grieve.
He calls the play *society*.
Some of his subjects really care
For all the broken-in heads,
Some cheer hungrily, while others
Pay no attention at all, desultory
On the outskirts, breathing blessings,
Yelling out curse words, or trying
To regain control of the animals
Running without reins. Eventually,
Everyone fractures in the stampede.
Somehow, no one climbs the wall
Or softens the earth or builds a net
Or puts an arrow in the king's eye

No matter how high the tide of shells
In their thousands, in their millions,
Washing up against the stones.
I want to say that today I will refuse
To break, that I will put the saviours
Out of a job and so crash this economy,
But I fear that I, like you, have mistaken
My role in this story—I am no more
And no less than the king's soft eye
Begging for the swift hit of a steel point.

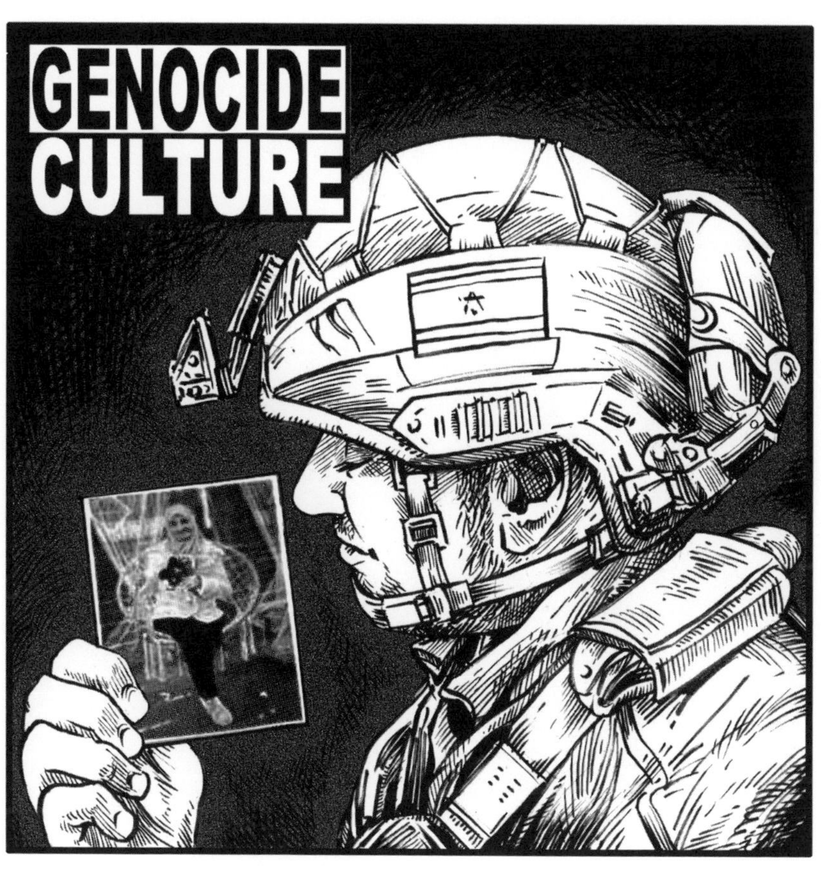
GENOCIDE
CULTURE

Trees in the genocide

After Hayan Charara's 'Animals'

In Falastin, a million trees became ash.
In Lebanon, 60 000 olive trees burn.
The soil burns too, and with it, the future.
When I blink, I see smoke flood over family.
This is a tragedy for the ages, and it does not rate
Here in the orchards of carnage. This poem-to-be
I give to the felled stumps. Dear leaf and fruit,
Allow me first to ode my human loves,
All the frail bodies in the places we home,
Those who offer a hand or eye to the maimed,
Who gently brush a giggling child's hair,
All our uncountable selves unmoored, stewards
Of the river and the sea, the stone and green.
When I am done kneeling to the people
Of Bilad al-Sham, I will return, I swear
To sing of your undoing, the poisoning of
Root and acorn, blessed bird and worm,
For the moon to mourn, if no one else.
Forgive me if this takes forever.

Pets in the genocide

For Mohammad Bhar

Man's best friend
Bled him, as trained.
Having never spoken,
Neither could explain
What was happening.
He was in his home.
Hey boy. Hey you.
Agony, a stranger,
Prowled the living
Room. They left him
To die alone. Forced
His mother away
And all who cared.
Hey boy. Hey you.
Each word a miracle
Amid the growling.
Khalas, habibi.

300 days in the genocide

I genocide everything
In the poem: this
        Blunt angel,
Real shadow,
        A tear in me

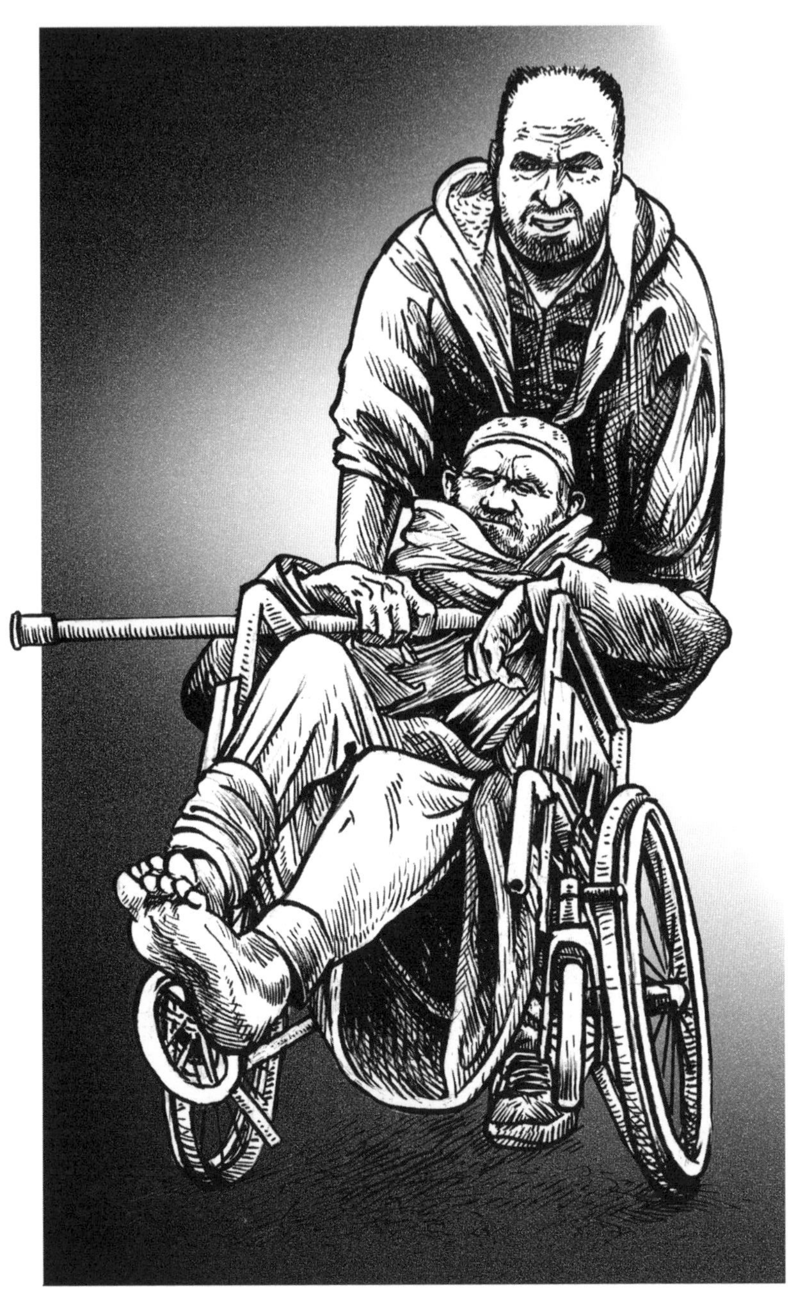

Father's Day in the genocide (reprise)

My father, the blade, I wield in verse
To redefine what is tolerable,
To sharpen my voice.
Swing, Baba! Change my name
To love, to who I arch for, the body
I paradise. O broken door!
Remember to ask, what is peace
At the point of a blade?
What is a father absent a mother?
What is a people absent love?
What is a son absent a land?
A hurt wind, a marred finale,
A prophet of blame.

GENOCIDE CULTURE
Israeli settlers sabotage aid trucks...
Intended for starving Gazans.

Democracy in the genocide

As we watch the dead heap and the living
Dwindle, the crowds rush to the ballot
Box. Later, they whisper, ashamed
Or defiantly proud, they voted for
The 'lesser' of two genocides
One real, and one possible.
A greater evil is imagined.
Hard as it is to fathom,
We can do worse, yes?
This pleases them.
I voted for this!
They proclaim,
You should be
Grateful.

Devastation in the genocide

After Fady Joudah

Fady, I checked on her as you instructed.
We call each other mother, you know
She produced me as I produce her.
In the garden where she weeps
Tears as large and audacious as cities—
Between Qalamoun and Al Quds,
Between Sydney and Syria—I ask her
Why have you not destroyed my enemy?
Did his invitation get lost in the mail?
What do you mean he is here too
With a sombre mien and damp napkin?
My god. Get out! Get out all of you!
Get all of me out! Mother, O mother
You have no purpose other than love,
Like any poem. I try to make this human,
Fool that I am, married to undying myth.
Didn't God warn not to look at what we
Wrought, with a pillar of womanly salt?
My mother's tongue clarifies: only
the martyr is a witness, and their words
Do not speak for us, but against.

Poetry in the genocide

To the limbless child, and the haunted eyes; to the charismatic boy smiling despite, and the scalped toddler in his father's arms or a man's arms, anyway—and anyone holding together the torn-apart child is a father in that moment I swear to God—; to the frustrated, the enraged, the wailing, the numb, the exhausted, to every hand with a lidless gaze recording their most intimate ruin, their relentless loving, for the indifferent clouds and the useless masses, I have to say: welcome to poetry, and I'm sorry, amid the universe of indignities, that this was ever called *porn*. A label given not to the giddy politicians bending over to sign missiles, but the rendering of the victims' refusal to vanish into the rubble. No, habibi, this is poetry, and I would not wish poetry upon anyone. Poetry salutes the dirt filling up the mass graves, and shrouds the dead solemnly, and rots in the mouth of the soldier. Poetry fails daily, laughs, and gets up again with a cracked face. Poetry opens your whole wretched spirit, and keeps opening, until you know yourself with an exactitude that only the divine can bear without collapse, and not a thing can stop it. Everyone in Palestine is a poet: O you have shown us ourselves, and this is a wound from which there can be no recovery.

We lived unhappily in the genocide

Against Ilya Kaminsky

I wash my son in the bathtub, alert
not to his body but the possibility
of harm, all the ways he might slip
and slam on tiles or curved ceramic lip.
He is joy incarnate and I cannot see him.
All the other children are here, waiting
to be washed by more than ethnic
cleansing. Outside, my pregnant love
rests swollen ankles, aching with future.
What shall we call you, O future? Each day,
another martyr is announced, and I mouth
their names against you, my buried punch
my sweet Hamza, Haniyeh, Yahya, Omar,
to see which clipped syllable reflects you.
Nothing fits. I shake our exhausted family
tree but Arabic is a haunted litany now
and only death falls out. My son,
O my son I cannot see you at all.

Sumud in the genocide

For Saadi Hassan Barakeh & Abu Saher al-Maghari

You ask how I can write in a time like this.
In Gaza, the gravedigger wakes with the light
and strives until night, hard at his craft, to gift
what remains to the dirt with a dignity denied
them in life. He remembers the dead by name
even now, twenty thousand shovel heaps later.
Here is the Laghi family, this is Abu Hasanein's
and there is Abu Hattab. Drones buzz dizzied
around the pooled bodies, like bees to honey
and in the distance the hive hums with glee.
All the cemeteries are filled, the dead buried
on the dead, masses on masses, yet he stands
under the sun, patient with his hands, and you
ask how I can write, as if this is difficult. How
can I not? How can I do any less than mark
all the hands at work, the rescuers and
their plastic bags, the donkey and the cart
piled with once-was, Abu Saher al-Maghari
shrouding each body at Al-Aqsa Martyrs
in white page after white page & finally,
Saadi, the gravedigger, the last to touch
the lost before the earth's rough welcome?
I think of Heaney's pen, the one he used to dig.
How it isn't close to enough. I snap the pen.
Give me a spade, God, give me a spear.

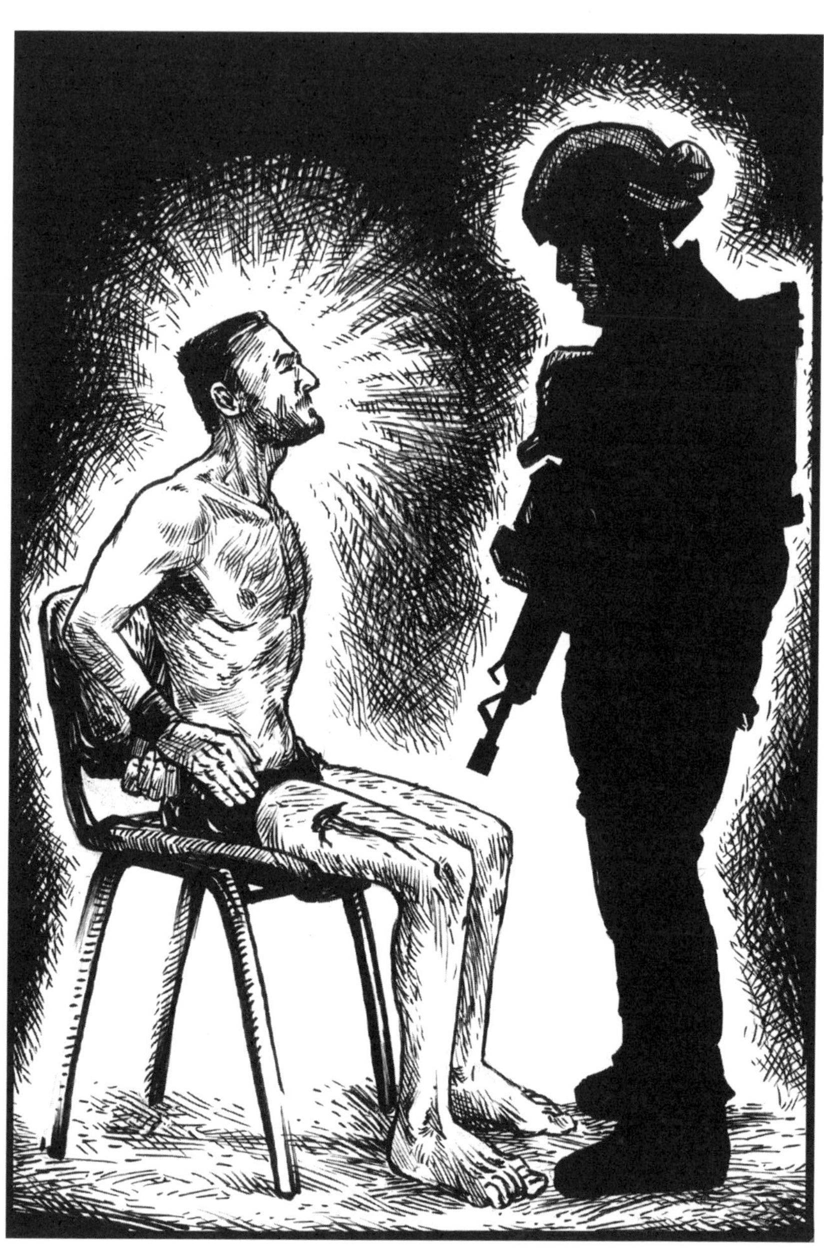

Dehumanised in the genocide

Arabs aren't people, they say.
I delight in this for I have seen
What people do. I do not
Want to be among them.
Let me die an Arab, a sore
Animal hungry for God—
Or any measure of grace.

Privilege in the genocide

In the morgue, my baby cousin
Whose first breath was final,
Lay still, a life I could cup in one.
I have not moved from this,
Nor will I. I was lucky to see him
So briefly. Another privilege: I
Held my grandmother's hand
As she took her last breath.
I kissed her ghost bismillah.
I closed her eyes and her eyes
Will stay with me until I depart.
Every minute another video offers
A view of death without love
Which is how I define apocalypse.
This much I can offer you:
My feet are rooted in sorrow-tilled
Fields. I know how to hold us,
The dead, the failures, the glories.
& when I don't, I tell necessary lies.
Our enemies fail to understand.
They razed all the cemeteries
In a futile frenzy to injure dirt
And time. Habibi, we are eternal.
We can enter loss from anywhere.
Both of my graves, here and there,
Remain alive in me. Maybe we
Should stop talking about the earth
As if there is an earth: it's memory
We inhabit, nothing you can keep.

Notes on the art

Some of these drawings reference historical images and documentary footage found in online news feeds and on social media, uneasily reflecting my status as a far-flung observer—a migrant and settler on the traditional lands of the Guringai people in Sydney, Australia. I pay my deepest respects to the traditional owners of the land on which these images were drawn, acknowledging that sovereignty was never ceded. I hope this book contributes to a growing culture of resistance and solidarity with Palestinian people, in their struggle for freedom, dignity, decolonisation and justice.

'Child amputee' (p. 13): This image was drawn from a photograph of Ghazal, a four-year-old whose family home was hit by Israeli artillery on 12 October 2023. UNICEF reported that a severe injury to Ghazal's left leg required emergency surgery under inadequate conditions and without anaesthesia. This led to an infection that precipitated the amputation of her leg some days later at the al-Nasser Hospital in Khan Younis. The UN children's agency states that more than 1000 children had one or more of their limbs amputated during the first two months of Israel's invasion in 2023.

'Genocide Culture' is a series of images that attempts to highlight what our leaders cannot be brought to admit: that a 'close friend' of Australia, a mutual ally of the United States and a key strategic partner in global security and military technology is committing the most abhorrent crime humanity is capable of. It will take a serious moral reckoning and reconciliation with Australia's own (frequently suppressed) colonial history before this country has the wherewithal to recognise and denounce the genocide committed by a fellow settler colony.

'Sarafand al-Amr' (p. 38) references the massacre of Palestinian villagers in Sarafand al-Amr in 1918 by 200 men from the ANZAC Mounted Division, alongside Scottish troops. The soldiers surrounded and burned the village, killing 40 Arab men. No one was ever prosecuted for the killings.

The images **'Lingerie'** (p. 20), **'Prisoners'** (p. 55), **'A child's bicycle'** (p. 60), **'Tank shell'** (p. 74) and **'An intimate moment'** (p. 133) are drawn from photographs and video that Israeli soldiers have uploaded to social media platforms, expressing mockery and celebration of the destruction visited upon the people and environment of Gaza.

'Child prisoner' (p. 64) is drawn from media footage showing the arrest of Palestinian children in the West Bank.

'Fatima' (p. 40): Fatima is a nine-year-old girl from Beit Hanoun. She was interviewed with her pet bird for *Eye on Palestine* in the al-Shati refugee camp in June 2024.

'Resistance' (p. 52): My drawing renders a Palestinian elder who was filmed in Jenin in September 2024, after an Israeli military incursion caused significant damage to local infrastructure, destroying roads as well as electricity and water connections. The man, whose identity wasn't disclosed, proudly raised the Palestinian flag and decried imperialist aggression to the journalist Sodqi Rayan. According to the United Nations Office for the Coordination of Humanitarian Affairs, 1004 Palestinians (including 213 children) in the West Bank were killed by Israel from January 2023 to December 2024, while 16,104 Palestinians (including 2503 children) were injured and 2946 structures (mostly homes) were destroyed.

'Samih Madhoun' (p. 56): A young musician and composer living in the Gaza Strip, Samih Madhoun was studying at the Edward Said National Conservatory of Music and would frequently perform there. After his family were forced to leave their destroyed home in Gaza City, Samih has played to displaced Gazans in the Deir al-Balah camp. In June 2024, he released an album on Bandcamp, *Oud Music from Gaza*, featuring his performances in the encampment among family and friends.

'Sderot Cinema' (p. 66) refers to the improvised viewing area made up of couches and chairs on a hilltop in the Israeli settlement of Sderot, which was built on the depopulated Palestinian village of Najd, located 6.5 kilometres from the Gaza Strip. Since 2009, locals have gathered to watch the Israeli army's bombing of Gaza, whooping and applauding when explosions are witnessed.

'Bisan Owda' (p. 70): With enormous heart and steadfastness, Bisan Owda has documented the daily experience of living under conditions of aerial bombardment, siege, displacement, deprivation of resources and genocide. A journalist, activist and filmmaker, Bisan's video and livestream reports describe and reflect on her own fast-changing circumstances and those of the people around her, giving powerful documentation and narrative force to the lives of Gazan civilians. That Bisan's reportage has gained an international audience numbering tens of millions underlines the inadequacy of traditional media outlets, which have largely ignored Palestinian voices in service of erasing or downplaying Israel's crimes against humanity.

Hind al-Rajab (p. 77): On 29 January 2024, five-year-old Hind al-Rajab travelled in the family car of her maternal uncle, Bashar Hamada, alongside his wife, Ana'am, and their four children, Layan, Raghad, Sarah and Mohammad. The family were leaving their home in Tel al-Hawa, which had been under heavy bombardment the night before, when their vehicle was struck by machine-gun fire from an Israeli tank. That assault killed everyone in the car except Hind and her fifteen-year-old cousin, Layan. In a phone call to the Palestinian Red Crescent Society, Layan could be heard asking for help before rapid machine-gun fire ended her life. Over the next few hours, as she sat among her dead relatives, Hind spoke to Red Crescent operators and her mother, begging them to rescue her. An ambulance was dispatched to retrieve her that evening after waiting on approval from Israeli authorities. That vehicle was shelled by an Israeli tank when it arrived at the location, killing two paramedics, Yusuf al-Zeino and Ahmed al-Madhoun. Hind and her six family members were found dead in their car twelve days later, after Israeli forces had left the area.

'A child in Berlin' (p. 88): This drawing references video footage from September 2024 in which the German police chased and detained a ten-year-old boy holding a Palestinian flag at a protest rally in Berlin.

'Teddy' (p. 90): This drawing references images uploaded to social media by Israeli soldiers who have decorated their military vehicles with the toys of killed or displaced Palestinian children. The Caterpillar D9 armoured bulldozer used by the Israel military (and supplied by Caterpillar Inc.) is nicknamed 'Teddy Bear'.

Hamada Shaqoura (p. 94): Hamada Shaqoura is a Gazan food blogger who uploads cooking videos that creatively utilise the meagre rations of humanitarian food aid. His videos show the creation of dishes such as tacos, pizza and candied apples, made from the basic ingredients of flour, tinned meats, cheese and sugar. His meals are then distributed to the displaced children of Gaza's tent encampments, evoking their surprise and satisfaction. In March 2024, Oxfam reported 'catastrophic' levels of hunger and starvation in Gaza, which were the highest ever recorded in terms of the number of people affected and their percentage of the overall population. The world had never before witnessed such a rapid deterioration into widespread starvation, achieved by Israel's deliberate blockade of food, water and aid into Gaza.

'Sama Tabil with her mum' (p. 106): The eight-year-old Sama Tabil lost her hair due to intense psychological stress after Israeli forces targeted the camp in Rafah where her family were staying. She and her mother spoke to Al Jazeera in Khan Younis, where they were sheltering in August 2024.

'Soul of my soul: Khaled Nabhan and Reem' (p. 120): In late November 2023, millions of people viewed footage of Khaled Nabhan cuddling and farewelling the lifeless body of his granddaughter Reem, who he affectionately called 'the soul of my soul'. Israel had bombed their home in Deir al-Balah, killing three-year-old Reem and her five-year-old brother, Tarek. Nabhan's obvious devotion to Reem inspired an outpouring of grief online, including countless visual tributes by artists and others from around the world. Those images were to be circulated again when Khaled was killed by Israel fourteen months later in the Nuseirat refugee camp. The pictures of Khaled and Reem are a deeply moving expression of empathy and grief. Yet, taken collectively, I would also argue for their importance as images of resistance. In their online multiplication and sharing, such pictures mount a powerful counter-discourse to the erasure and demonisation of

Palestinian and Arab people (particularly men) after decades of racist and Islamophobic dehumanisation.

'Anas al-Sharif' (p. 128): A resident of the Jabaliyya refugee camp in northern Gaza, Al Jazeera journalist Anas al-Sharif has fearlessly reported Israel's crimes against Palestinian civilians. In December 2023, his family's house was bombed, killing his 90-year-old father. This follows a pattern of journalists and their families being threatened and targeted by the Israeli military. According to the International Federation of Journalists, at least 166 journalists and media workers were killed by Israel from October 2023 to January 2025, and several more are missing.

'The Great March of Return' (pp. 100–101): The Great March of Return (2018) was a beautiful act of organised, non-violent resistance, in which tens of thousands of Palestinians mobilised to protest Israel's thirteen-year land, sea and air blockade of the Gaza Strip, compounding decades of military occupation. The protest ended in Israeli snipers killing 266 people, including 50 children, and injuring over 30,000 more. Journalists and medical workers were among those killed. The drawing on page 100 is taken from footage of young Palestinians performing a traditional folk dance with accompanying Dabke. The facing image references a prosthetics specialist at the Artificial Limbs and Polio Centre in Gaza City. After the event, Israeli snipers spoke to *Haaretz* about the intentional wounding and disabling of Palestinian protesters, with one claiming to have shot 42 'knees' in a single day.

'Terrorism' (pp. 126–127): The journalist cited is *The Australian*'s chief international correspondent, Cameron Stewart.

'A scene from the al-Tabaeen massacre' (p. 145): This drawing references the aftermath of a bombing that took place on 10 August 2024, in which an Israeli air assault killed over 100 displaced Palestinians sheltering in the al-Tabaeen school in the al-Daraj area of Gaza City. So many bodies were dismembered beyond recognition that survivors and rescue workers collected the remains in plastic bags allocated by weight (70 kilograms per person), which were then given to family members for burial.

'Dawud' (p. 146): This image references the story of David (Dawud in Arabic) and Goliath. The figure of Dawud is based on a photograph (taken by Palestinian journalist Mahmud Hams) of Gaza resident Saber al-Ashqar. Al-Ashqar was photographed in his wheelchair with a slingshot at the Great March of Return on 11 May 2018. He had lost both his legs during Israeli's military invasion of Gaza in 2008.

The Lion of Gaza (p. 152): This drawing references a photograph of Hamza Abu Halima under interrogation in his underwear, tied to a chair and bleeding from his right leg. The picture was taken during a round-up of Palestinians in the Yarmouk area of Gaza City in December 2023. Shortly before that, Hamza's father, Khamis Abu Halima, was killed by the Israeli army along with Hamza's sister-in-law and her two children, Khamis (age six) and Haya (age three). The image was uploaded to social media by Yosee Gamzoo Letova, a photographer working for the Israeli forces, who jokingly referred to 'torturing a Palestinian civilian'. That attempt to humiliate Hamza backfired spectacularly as the image of his defiance went viral, fast becoming a source of pride among Palestinians.

Dr Safdar Ahmed

Author's note

Asalaamu alaikun. This book is a product of genocide, and as such it was important to me, and to my friend and collaborator Dr Safdar Ahmed, to dedicate all author royalties generated by sales of this book to Palestinian charities and relief efforts. I started writing this sequence of poems in late 2023 when I fractured my spine in a fall and was bed-bound, unable to attend the protests and actions I had been going to regularly. This was my attempt to turn my eyes, my heart, my gift, my labour and leverage, to recording what was being obscured from the outset. I was and remain completely depressed by the refusal of mainstream media to name the genocide, despite the distressing transparency of it, both as articulated by Israelis and shown to us by Palestinians on the ground, which is why I insisted on the inclusion of *genocide* in almost every title of this monstrous sequence. Let me be clear in saying that the monstrosity I reference is not just the subject matter, not just the horrors wreaked by the Western-armed and funded apartheid state, but also the evil of this witness: we are not apart from this, we are part of it.

At the time of writing, the official death toll in Gaza is said to stand at around 49,651 with over 100,000 wounded. 'Official', meaning, confirmed bodies that have been tagged and numbered in Gaza's devastated health system. Official, meaning, accepted by a Western establishment that is complicit in arming, funding, and providing political and propagandistic cover for the genocide itself. Official does not mean *real.* I am a student of language and its impacts; as a poet and a man and a Muslim it is my belief that the words we use are of spectacular importance in generating meaning, and as such enabling or inhibiting action. Take, for example, the innocuous and oft-repeated phrase 'death toll'—what does this imply? A natural occurrence, and a price that has to be paid; that is, an inevitability. Gaza does not have a death toll, it has a massacre manifest, a list of the murdered, a decimation resulting from genocide.

On 9 January 2025, *The Lancet* medical journal published a peer-reviewed analysis by epidemiologists at the London School of Hygiene and Tropical Medicine and academics at Yale University that concluded the estimated dead in Gaza had been undercounted by 41 per cent and therefore the real number of murdered individuals was likely to be 64,260 and could be as high as 78,525—this accounting ends as of 30 June 2024. So, 78,525 killed between October 7th and the end of June, or one in 35 inhabitants. This number includes only those 'directly' killed by Israeli forces, their bombs and bullets, shrapnel and debris.

'Indirect' deaths are not counted, nor cited by Western politicians, perhaps because an explanation would be required as to how, exactly, one dies indirectly. This definition includes anyone who dies from preventable illness, hunger etc.—a demarcation that is particularly useless in the context of a genocide perpetrated by Israeli officials and public figures who have repeatedly articulated their intent to destroy the entirety of Gaza; to cut off the food, water and electricity; to allow for the spread of diseases to cut through the populace; and who have systematically targeted hospitals, doctors, nurses, health centres, ambulances and paramedics.

Let us return to the figure of 78,525. Last year, *The Lancet* published a separate analysis that referenced a study on modern urban warfare that found 'indirect' killings in urban warfare were up to 15 times the number of 'direct' killings. The author suggested a conservative multiplication of four to arrive at a true estimation, then, of the number of people killed so far in Occupied Palestine: 78,525 times four equals 314,100. This is the conservative estimate, and it is in line with a projection by Professor Devi Sridhar (Chair of Global Public Health, University of Edinburgh), who in September 2024 wrote in *The Guardian* that she expected the number to reach half a million and certainly 335,500 by the end of 2024.

As nauseating and appalling as this is, we should also consider a non-conservative application of this study—what is the worst-case scenario here? The nonprofit Airwars, which analyses the impact of modern airstrikes, released a report proving that Israel's strikes in Gaza were unprecedented in their scope, intensity and casualty count. I quote: 'By almost every metric, the harm to civilians from the first month of the Israeli campaign in Gaza is incomparable with any 21st-century air campaign. It is by far the most intense, destructive, and fatal conflict for civilians that Airwars has ever documented.'

With this in mind, should we not at least consider what the highest end of this scale indicates, and multiply the estimated killed by 15 instead of four? This would leave us at 1.17 million (1,177,875) or roughly half the population murdered in a single year. I remind you that these figures are based on a confirmed 'death toll' that ends in June 2024. At the time of writing, we are seven months of bombings, starvation, torture, rape, summary executions and sniper shots down-wind from this figure. Irrespective of the final number, we are talking about a colossal loss of life and historic trauma that has reshaped the world into a smaller, uglier place. I highlight the scale only because it's important to understand, given how even the drastic undercount of 'directly' killed people is routinely denied by political and media figures, that the estimate of over 300,000 dead is in no way hyperbolic, but rather a measured accounting that does not approach the extreme end of possibility.

I am far from alone in asserting the reality of this genocide. On 4 December 2024, Amnesty International released a 300-page report detailing the crimes against humanity perpetrated by Israel and concluding it was genocide; on 19 December 2024, Human Rights Watch released their own 179-page report titled *Extermination and Acts of Genocide: Israel Deliberately Depriving Palestinians of Water*; both of these were preceded by Israeli historian Lee Mordechai's 124-page report of evidence, titled *Bearing Witness*, which came out in January 2024, and Forensic Architecture's 827-page report, *A Cartography of Genocide*. In July 2024, the International

Court of Justice issued a ruling finding Israel guilty of racial segregation and apartheid against Palestinians, and in November, the International Criminal Court issued arrest warrants against Israeli Prime Minister Benjamin Netanyahu and his now-former defence minister, Yoav Gallant, for crimes against humanity.

The evidence is clear; the reality is undeniable. This book is dedicated not just to the Palestinians who have been murdered and, even in their mass graves, still find their existence subjected to a racist debate, but to those who live—nobody questions the figure of over 100,000 wounded because the living, trapped in the Gaza Strip, pose no risk to the status quo the way the legal definition of genocide does, however minimally. Nobody questions that Israel and the West have collectively created the largest cohort of child amputees in history; indeed, the practice of deliberately disabling and maiming Palestinians is long established by Israel. The daily immiseration of Palestinians in the brutal reality of apartheid is unquestioned, and no urgency is given to their relief and liberation.

Insha'Allah this book, even if it is only one grain of sand, will help tip the scales toward justice for the living and the dead, the disappeared and the displaced and all who remain. May we all live to see a free Palestine.

Salaam,
Omar

Acknowledgements

Firstly, I would like to thank my Palestinian comrades who have been so steadfast in articulating and resisting the violently racist constraints of empire, particularly George Abraham, whose insights have been so important to my thinking and living, and whose friendship I cherish; likewise Najwan Darwish, whose words grace this book, and who is a beloved presence in my life. I have so much love for these Palestinian writers, who I've been lucky enough to work with or to know in some capacity through organising, and through letters: Naomi Shihab Nye, Tariq Luthun, Noor Hindi, Rasha Abdulhadi, Summer Farah. And of course, where would I be without the foundational guidance provided by the works of Edward Said and Ghassan Kanafani? Nowhere worth mentioning. Shoutout as well to Fady Joudah and Lena Khalaf Tuffaha, for no reason other than I love their work, and you, dear reader, must go and read their books.

Thank you to Create NSW, for the grant that supported this important collaboration with Safdar Ahmed; thank you to Safdar, my brother in Islam, for your exemplary work in this book and elsewhere, you are an extraordinary man whose humility and compassion I can only hope to mirror; and to my publisher Aviva Tuffield at UQP, whose support has been so vital to me personally and professionally.

I would especially like to honour every one of the more than 200 murdered Palestinian journalists, and the unknown number of Palestinian citizen journalists, who continued—in the face of overwhelming horror and overwhelming apathy from world leaders—to document the evils committed against them. Though the genocide did not stop, you made so many marks in hearts around the world; you are stamped in mine and throughout this book: it was not for nought, and we will not forget, this I swear.

This book was written and conceived on the lands of the Dharug people, where I was born and raised, and I extend my respect and love to their Elders and, through them, to the lands and waters and air that have sustained me and my family, and continue to do so. Sovereignty was never ceded, and our debt to Country, our obligation to dismantle the oppressive colonial system, is enormous and ongoing. May we see reparations, treaty, and the end of the hideously entrenched anti-Indigenous racism and disadvantage that continues to plague the original inhabitants and custodians of this land.

Love,
Omar